MW00452656

THE GREAT SEPARATION

THE GREAT SEPARATION

A History
of the Separation of the United States
into Two Independent Republics
in 2029

by JOHN DOE, Ph.D.

(At the request of the Department of Homeland Security, the author's true identity is concealed)

ROYA PUBLICATIONS

THE GREAT SEPARATION

Copyright © 2016 Roya Publications
Registration Number: TX 8-226-937
February 16, 2016

Published by Roya Publications
Newbury Park, CA
www.royapublications.com

Cover Design by Mandana Khoshnevisan

All Rights Reserved. No part of this book may be reproduced or transmitted in any form or by electronic or mechanical means, including photographic and other information storage and retrieval systems, without written permission by the publisher, except by a reviewer who may quote passages in a review.

For more information, contact info@royapublications.com

ISBN: 978-1-944218-08-9 (trade paperback)
ISBN: 978-1-944218-04-1 (trade paperback)
ISBN: 978-1-944218-00-3 (electronic)

ACKNOWLEDGMENTS

In absence of acknowledgements from the Author,
the Publisher gratefully acknowledges important contributions
from Mandy Marvelle and Michael Photo-Magique; helpful reviews
from Sharan Splendide, Tara Très-Coole, and Bev Bodaciouse, as well
as meticulous editing by Ed Exacto. (Real names withheld for
national security reasons.)

CONTENTS

PUBLISHER'S NOTE 1

PREFACE 3

PART ONE: SEPARATION 5

    Chapter One: Introduction to Separation (Red vs. Blue) 7

    Chapter Two: The Great Separation 31

    Chapter Three: What Happened Here? 39

    Chapter Four: Two New Countries? 47

PART TWO: SIBLING RIVALRY 77

    Chapter Five: First Steps to New Government 79

    Chapter Six: The Separation Committee (Or, Dividing the
    Assets) 117

PART THREE: LIVING WITH CHANGE 125

Chapter Seven: Life Apart 127

Chapter Eight: Life on the Borders 153

Chapter Nine: Separation or Divorce? 159

AFTERWORD 163

APPENDICES 169

Appendix One: Country Relocation Algorithm 171

Appendix Two: A Country Divided 175

Appendix Three: Timeline 203

ABOUT THE AUTHOR 209

PUBLISHER'S NOTE

PUBLICATION OF THIS HISTORICAL DOCUMENT has been facilitated by the publisher's use of an experimental product called "FutureView" (or FuVu), which, on the few occasions when it works, allows one to link to and download documents from the future. As luck would have it, we stumbled upon a manuscript from late 2029, written by historian Dr. John Doe [real name withheld for security reasons]. In his writing, he describes the dramatic events surrounding the 2028 presidential election and its aftermath in 2029, provided here as a historical perspective. For national security reasons, the publisher cannot provide any details of how it gained access to the highly restricted technology that created FuVu.

While denying rumors that Google® (a part of Alphabet Inc.) is the main developer of FuVu, Google and its affiliates emphasize that they assume no responsibility for any inaccuracies in depicting the future in any of their products. They further insist that all inaccuracies in their future vision devices, if they should have any, will be corrected in the software's version 2.0, which will be available in early 2029.

PREFACE

Dateline: Fall 2029

In a few months, people in a country that used to be called the United States of America will be celebrating the first anniversary of the division of that country into two independent republics: the American Republic of Compassion (ARC) and the Armed Christian Nations of America (ACNA). The separation has not been easy, and it certainly does not seem complete. But based on the first year's experience, it does seem as though it may be this permanent separation that has brought peace and tranquility to the people living in these two republics.

According to many political and cultural analysts, the separation is indeed real and irreversible. Many — both academics and laypeople — wonder why it did not happen earlier.

The purpose of this book is to analyze the social, economic and political dynamics that caused one of the most stable democracies in the world to experience a bloodless social revolution, which, according to many scholars and historians, will prove more significant than the French and Russian revolutions in terms of shaping our world.

Given the fact that the separation, at the moment I write this preface, is barely one year old, no doubt there will be additional facts and documents that will become available in the coming years. A more cautious historian would wait a few more years before providing analyses and explanations. But while waiting a few years might indeed benefit from the availability of additional documents and facts, it might also impact the memories and firsthand knowledge of some of the main participants.

Therefore, in a bold attempt, and yet with a certain level of professional humility, this monograph provides an early analysis of what happened in the United States of America in the early 21st century that resulted in this schism. I have used both primary and secondary sources. Given the fact that many of the major events that I discuss in this book are only a few months old, I have used original documents and press releases as source material whenever possible. I have decided that, instead of trying to interpret the events or intentions, I will let the reader arrive at his or her own judgment. No doubt future editions of this book will provide a more comprehensive analysis of the events and forces that contributed to the division of the United States of America in 2029 — almost a century after another defining moment in U.S. history. This time however, it was not a Great Depression; rather, it was a Great Separation.

John Doe, Ph.D.
Professor of Contemporary American History
Institute for Advanced Studies
Las Vegas, Nevada

PART ONE

Separation

"On Monday, November 20, 2028, at exactly 9:00 a.m., the Supreme Court convened to hear *Faith v. Castro*. At exactly 11:05 a.m., the world changed forever."

CHAPTER ONE

"A working person that supports Democrats is like a chicken that supports Col. Sanders!"

- Bumper sticker (Kansas City)

"ANNOY A REPUBLICAN: Be honest. Do good. Help people."

- Bumper sticker (San Francisco)

SINCE THE FOUNDING OF THE United States of America in 1776, Americans[1] had been politically and socially divided. However, to the extent that there were truly national ideological divisions, I argue that for most of the country's history, such disagreements were not about the ends, but rather about the means of achieving the ends.

The first British colonists arrived on the Mayflower at what would become Plymouth, Massachusetts, and that ship was only the first of many to bring British colonists — and many other immigrants — to

---

1   Forgive my imprecise language; I am referring here to the denizens of the previously united United States. Technically, living on the American continent, we all continue to be "Americans."

what would become the United States of America.[2] Then, for over two hundred years, Americans managed to steer the ship of state in a unified manner. But eventually, the shipmates could no longer agree on a course, and there was — not a mutiny, but a parting of the ways. The ship and its crew were both split in half. What made them choose this drastic course, and will the two halves of the ship sink, or improbably continue to sail? Only time can tell. I can but examine what has happened thus far.

Furthermore, what rock did this ship of state strike that caused an actual crack to form? Plenty of other countries have sailed through stormy seas for hundreds of years without splitting apart. There are plenty of events and explanations that I will attempt to outline and explain, but I do feel that perhaps the final blow was an accident. Just as it may be said that concepts do not exist in a people's minds until their language contains a word for it,[3] perhaps these two diametrically opposed concepts of Red and Blue were not fully part of our thought process until our media — and therefore our country — accidentally defined these terms for the people. This accident happened in November of 2000, specifically on the night of the presidential election of George W. Bush.

Before that very moment in our media's history there had been no consistent or standardized color symbolic systems in place to refer to ideology. But then came the 2000 election between Bush and Al Gore. This election's results remained unsettled for several days. During this time of uncertainty, there was virtually round-the-clock

---

2   Of course, there were many people already living here long before that. Those indigenous people were also divided up into smaller nations, rather than being unified across the whole land. Perhaps we have returned to the most sensible model, after all.

3   In George Orwell's *1984*, the government seeks to manage the people's way of thinking, not by adding words, but rather by taking them away: ""'Don't you see the whole aim of Newspeak is to narrow the range of thought? In the end we shall make thoughtcrime literally impossible, because there will be no words in which to express it. Every concept that can ever be needed will be expressed in exactly ONE word, with its meaning rigidly defined and all its subsidiary meanings rubbed out and forgotten" (1984, Chapter 5, Project Gutenberg Australia ewtext, http://gutenberg.net.au/ ebooks01/0100021.txt)

coverage of the issue, and everyone in the media was referring to the same election maps — so major media outlets started using the same colors consistently, for clarity in reporting. For the first time, the media endlessly discussed "red states" and "blue states" and everyone meant the same thing by it; by the time the prolonged media frenzy was over, the terminology had become national and permanent.

After the 2000 election, the designations simply stuck. Republican states were "Red States" and Democratic states were "Blue States." Perhaps it is not even that states and their people *were* more polarized after that election, but simply that by being consistently defined in the media in such stark terms, people *felt* more polarized. This one small accident of media may have been the rock that struck the ship of state and allowed it to split. We may never know. But there is a certain poetry in it. Nevertheless, I endeavor to argue it was in the early 21st century that the emergence of "Red" and "Blue" identities, so strongly defined and so far apart, sent the ship of the United States on two different trajectories, cracking apart — perhaps forever.

In writing this monograph, I must rely on historical documents to supply detailed information of events beyond my memory.[4] Further, even though the Great Separation has only happened mere months ago as of this writing, it is already difficult to track down historical documents and accounts that are politically neutral. Many have been archived or destroyed. Some people wonder whether they ever existed. Even more taxing: starting in the 2000s the amount of actual information is so vast, thanks to the advent of the internet, that sifting through it all, even with excellent search tools, proves taxing. Nevertheless, I shall endeavor to do my best in reconstructing the events of the Great Separation, tying it when possible to the reasons leading up to it.

---

4   Most of my historical information comes from Wikipedia, currently acknowledged as the most neutral and most reliable source of Pre-Separation United States history. And if the information turns out not to be strictly true, it may be enough that it feels true, or has appropriate levels of truthiness. Kudos here to Steven Colbert, for coining perhaps the most needed word of our century.

PRESIDENTIAL ELECTION 2028

"There is nothing which I dread so much as a division of the republic into two great parties, each arranged under its leader, and concerting measures in opposition to each other. This, in my humble apprehension, is to be dreaded as the greatest political evil under our Constitution."

- John Adams, circa 1800

BY THE BEGINNING OF THE second decade of the 21st century, it was clear that there was something definitely, irreversibly wrong with the American political system. Partisanship and sociopolitical polarization were endangering the health of the federal government, as well as its effectiveness in dealing with national and international crises. The American federal government as well as individual state governments were so unwilling to compromise over certain issues that they were forced into government shutdowns numerous times between 2012 and 2028. But no one seemed to make the connection between the political structure and culture of the country and its state of affairs — or if they did, they were mostly academics, to whom no one pays attention anyway.

The "last" American presidential primary elections before the Great Separation came in 2028.[5] After three forgettable presidential terms, where in each case the least offensive candidate had won, the 2028 candidate field began with the largest number of potential candidates of any previous presidential race — and from the most nontraditional parties.

Candidates began announcing their campaigns as early as 2026, and dropping out of the race just as quickly. There were several rappers, who each made a campaign music video to promote their respective new albums, although their real battle was against each other for record sales, so they soon stepped down from the race. Vermin Too, a political actor, ran a satirical and very unconventional campaign, reminiscent of the original Vermin Love Supreme (an actor and political prankster in early 2000's who ran repeatedly on a platform of "zombie apocalypse awareness, time travel research, and a free pony for every American.") Vermin Too's publicity-seeking campaign was short-lived. Famous drag queen/supermodel Ivana B'President ran on behalf of the Love Party, advocating for, mostly, love. Ms. Tanya Silverwood, from Taos, New Mexico, ran on behalf of the Freedom Party, with her only platform issue being the legalization of psychedelics, including peyote and LSD. Jeremiah Rockwell ran for The Rent is Too Damn High Party, which began as essentially a joke but achieved some minor but significant effectiveness finding low-income housing for the homeless. Some minor parties (the TLC party and the HGTV party, for example) held reality shows to select their candidates. There was also a strong campaign attempt by the Green Party, still soldiering on, like in many previous elections. Most of these fringe campaigns dropped out or otherwise disappeared well before 2028 began.

By early 2028, though the field was still wide, each party had narrowed its practical options to the two most viable candidates.

---

5   Of course, the actual primary process began in 2026, when the candidates began to zigzag across the country looking for money so they could finance their campaigns.

Among Democrats, the leading contenders were Senator Henry Castro (D, CA) and Cynthia Wong, governor of New York. The top Republican hopefuls were William Manchester, president of the National Rifle Association, and Christine Faith, governor of Texas. Faith was especially effective as the latest in a long parade of "Attila the Honeys" — attractive and extremely conservative female GOP spokespeople — a parade that stretched back to the early days of the 21st century and included Sarah Palin, Michelle Bachmann, Laura Ingraham and Ann Coulter.

There were also two major "outlier" candidates, who espoused the extreme political views of people at the edges of the spectrum. On the liberal side was Mandy Nasser, a civil-rights attorney from Eugene, Oregon. Nasser had gotten national attention some 20 years earlier when she spoke at demonstrations in Portland and Seattle that were related to the "Occupy Wall Street" movement.[6] She was backed by the Green Party and some Libertarian groups, and garnered considerable media attention. The most prominent far-right candidate was Paul Wallace IV, who professed to belong to the Tea Party, and whose political platform consisted of just one item: "Send non-Americans back to their countries." His campaign brochure provided more detail about candidate Wallace's geopolitical position. Under a photo of Wallace at a backyard barbecue, wearing a stars-and-stripes apron with a bald eagle on it, flipping burgers at the grill with his family smiling in the background, was the text:

America is for Americans. We cannot allow non-Americans to pollute our cultural purity and that is why, in January 2029, when

---

6   The protests, largely in response to the situation leading to the 2007 financial collapse, began in New York City on September 17, 2011. Soon there were similar protests across the United States. (The movement's structure — and timing — was similar to the Tea Party's, in that protests were local and organized by members; also, some participants in local protests had agendas that had little to do with the stated meaning of the protests. The difference was, the Tea Party was extremely right wing and nationally funded/organized from behind the scenes by the Koch brothers, whereas the Occupy movement was a left-wing movement and was nationally funded/organized by … no one at all.)

I am sworn in as the president of the United States of America, I will send all non-Americans back to where they came from.

I will send African-Americans back to Africa, American Indians back to India, the Italians back to Italy, the Irish back to Ireland, the Persians back to France, and the Saudis back to Monte Carlo. All Spanish-speaking people will go back to Spain.

Yes. America is only for Americans.

Given Wallace's simple but extreme position, which gave even some hardline conservatives pause, and the refusal of Mandy Nasser to accept corporate donations (and limiting individual donations to $5), it became clear early in the campaign that neither of them was a serious contender in the presidential race.

So once again, the presidential campaign was a contest between the Democratic and the Republican parties: two parties and their candidates with two different views of America's priorities and concerns; two different views of the American people and their needs and their dreams. It was jail versus college. It was bombers and aircraft carriers versus schools and hospitals. It was drilling and fracking versus conservation and renewable energy. On both sides, the remaining two candidates were solid examples of the hopes and dreams of their party. America did not know it then, but they were engaged in casting the leading characters in a very unexpected political drama that would change, perhaps, the entire world.

The Blues: Castro vs. Wong

The Democratic Party had two excellent candidates to choose from, both of whom symbolized, according to the party, "the future of America."

Primary election results favored California's Senator Henry Castro. A California native born to undocumented farmworkers in the Central Valley, the 58-year-old Castro began his career as an assistant professor in the College of Ethnic Studies at San Francisco State University, after receiving his Ph.D. at the University of California, Berkeley. As a professor he was extremely popular with students, and his classes usually had a long waiting list.

After receiving tenure at SFSU, he began his political and community involvement which culminated in his election as mayor of the city of San Francisco. He moved quickly to state senate, then the U.S. Senate, where he became known for his commitment to social justice and environmental issues.

Senator Castro seemed like the perfect candidate. He exuded friendliness: he was a relatively short man, balding, and with a whimsical handlebar mustache cropped in such a way as to look like a slight smile, even at rest. His students found him "relatable," "charming," "frickin' hilarious," and "easy to talk to." Among colleagues, he was known for his sharp intellect and his sense of humor. He was seen as a champion for science, technology and innovation. The only issue that had the potential to cause him political problems with the opposing party was the fact that, some seven years earlier, he had married his longtime companion, Jack Gorbanski, a software engineer at Apple's headquarters in Cupertino, California. Though gay rights had progressed enormously in recent years, and Gorbanski was a model citizen who would make an excellent First Gentleman,[7] the Democratic Party elders were not sure whether the majority of Americans were ready to elect their first gay president.

Governor Cynthia Wong, Castro's fiercest opponent, was herself the daughter of two immigrants, and she had a similar rags-to-riches backstory which also appealed to believers in the American Dream.

---

7 Gorbanski was also a child of immigrants: his parents grew up in the Ukraine. Gorbanski had grown up in Massachusetts and had attended MIT as an undergraduate majoring in computer science and fine arts.

Both of Wong's parents emigrated from Taiwan to the United States in 1972. They owned a Chinese restaurant in what was once known as Little Italy, which by the early 1970s had become the heart of New York City's Chinatown.

Governor Wong had attended public schools in New Jersey and graduated from Baruch College before attending law school at night, while working as a high school social science teacher in Brooklyn. Upon graduating, she joined New York City's Public Defender's Office where she successfully defended several high-profile cases. After a few years, she joined the District Attorney's Office and was quickly promoted to the position of assistant district attorney. Upon the retirement of the previous district attorney, she ran for the position and was elected. The D.A. position provided her with exposure and publicity to run for the state Senate and eventually for the governor's seat. She had been in the position for only three years at the time of the 2028 presidential primaries.

Wong's image in the press was one of stylish, urban sophistication. Sporting a sleek bob, she was also famous for her candy-color pantsuits, with silhouettes and details that gave slightly more than a nod to the sixties fashions of Jackie Kennedy. A very short woman, "five-two in stocking feet," as she freely admitted, she inevitably wore sky-high heels. Asked about her signature footwear choice by people.com, Wong laughed, "I like to be able to look my competition in the eye. I probably can't climb a mountain in these ... but I *can* run." Wong was married to Reginald Smith, who was the owner of a Harlem jazz club. They had two teenage children — Zora and Langston — who were in high school at the time of the 2028 primaries.

As the most diverse set of Democratic presidential candidates to date, they mutually agreed behind the scenes to run a clean campaign: no ads bashing each other, only the Republicans. As the election neared, polling and primary election results favored Castro over Wong. One notable liberal blogger was known to grumble, "Of course there'll be a gay male president before a Chinese woman." But in general, Blue America was pleased with the available choices and with the outcome.

The Reds: Faith vs. Winchester

On the Red side, of the two viable candidates, there was a clear frontrunner: Governor Christine Faith, from Houston, Texas. Her polished appearance and no-nonsense governing — and the fact that she was the most sensible female candidate the Republican Party had ever nominated — made her a relative shoo-in. Governor Faith was already well-known to the public, since she had been the governor of Texas for more than 10 years. Even before her national candidacy, during her time as governor she appeared frequently onscreen as a Republican spokesperson on national and international issues. Faith was an instantly recognizable screen presence. Her blond hair was usually piled into a sleek updo, and her rimless glasses had red temples. She was almost never seen in public wearing pants, except when she and her husband were out riding horses on their ranch. Her husband, Justin Faith,[8] came from an oil family, and together Christine and Justin and their four children (Matthew, Mark, Luke, and Nicole) lived on a spacious ranch just outside of Houston.

Faith's selection as presidential candidate was a calculated response to the public outcry that Reds systematically ignored women's rights. Indeed, Republicans opposed such things as reproductive rights and equal pay for women. But with such an attractive, well-spoken, accomplished woman potentially at the head of their ticket, they hoped Faith's presence would give Republican women enough confidence to vote for her. For once, the Republican Party's bid to appeal to women had a chance of actually succeeding.

William Winchester, from Helena, Montana, was the runner-up candidate in most of the primaries. He was a former Montana

---

8   Her choice to take her husband's last name was controversial to some women, though she countered, "When given the opportunity to take the name Faith, how could I refuse?"

senator and president of the National Rifle Association. He was very popular with both Libertarians and far-right Republicans, which was a definite advantage in the race. Winchester had adopted the strategy of the historic John McCain/Sarah Palin campaign, proudly claiming himself to be a maverick. He often wore cowboy boots and ten-gallon hats with his suits for political events, and had a collection of patriotic belt buckles; he was always proud to show off that day's buckle to the press at the slightest opportunity. A commonly shouted "last question" at press conferences was, "What are you wearing?" and Winchester was always happy to indulge. Indeed, he made a point to buy a new buckle at every campaign stop during the 2028 race; it made for a good meet-and-greet with local small-business owners.

He also, however, had a reputation for having a quick temper. As a senator, on more than one occasion he had challenged a fellow senator who disagreed with him to a gunfight in front of the Lincoln Memorial. No one had taken him up on his offer yet. But on his scheduled gunfight days, and many others, despite protest from the Senate sergeant-at-arms, he carried his pistol with him into the Senate's chamber.

Also slightly worrisome to Republican Party elders: Winchester was unmarried. Only six presidents had ever been elected while unmarried, and only two of those had never been married before — and those were both Democrats![9] An unmarried president, fretted Republicans, would not be the best representation of family values. On the other hand, party officials mused, the search for a wife for Winchester would certainly be good publicity — a few even suggested a reality show to find the winning spouse.

The Conventions: Choosing Our Candidates

---

9   Thomas Jefferson, Martin Van Buren, Chester A. Arthur, and Andrew Jackson were all widowers when elected president. Democrats James Buchanan and Grover Cleveland had never been married before being elected president. Cleveland married while in office; Buchanan stayed unmarried till the end of his life.

By this time in American history, of course, national conventions were purely political theater, part rally and part platform development — though some of us dimly recall that a mere fifty or sixty years earlier, the presidential and vice presidential candidates were actually chosen at the convention through real-time voting by delegates. By the late 20th century, however, candidates were essentially already decided by the end of the primary elections in early June. The conventions were thus places where party leaders generated support for candidates and helped to develop the party's platform for the general elections.

Blues

The Democratic National Convention was held in Chicago on July 24-27, 2028. More than 40,000 delegates, guests, journalists, observers and activists went to the Windy City to participate, observe, report and express their opinions.

The Democratic Party was withholding of its insider information, but the leaders must have worked hard behind the scenes to make things go as planned during the convention. During the primary campaigns, the party worked very hard to make Senator Castro's sexual orientation a non-issue, and according to both official transcripts and one-on-one interviews, it was not brought up at the convention. However, every night during the convention, which was televised on nearly all the major networks, Fox News instead devoted the entire time to sermons and commentary on the subject of homosexuality.

The Democratic Party platform adopted on the last night of the convention included a commitment to social justice, tax reform, gun control, environmental preservation, freedom of choice (i.e., abortion rights), and equal pay for women.[10]

---

10 A few delegates tried to include campaign finance reform in the platform. But the item did not generate enough support and it was not included in the final version. It seems that as far as campaign finance was concerned, there was not much of a difference between the two parties.

As the convention was approaching, Castro had a very slight edge over Governor Wong; the number of uncommitted delegates could have made the convention rather messy. But in late June, after both candidates attended a retreat at the home of Apple's CEO, much of which was clandestine apart from a very public photo session in the lush garden out back, Governor Wong publicly threw her support to Senator Castro, who in return selected Wong as his running mate. A major political crisis was thus aborted, and the convention delegates were able to nominate Castro for president.

Reds

The Republican National Convention of 2028 took place in Kansas City, Missouri. By the time of the convention in early August, everyone already knew who the presidential choice was going to be. As she was ahead in the primaries and backed by a wide swath of American conservatives, the Republicans had clearly chosen Christine Faith, Texas governor and GOP darlin'.

But what had not yet been decided was who Governor Faith's running mate would be. There were several contenders. Among them were two individuals who seemed to be the front-runners. The first was William Winchester, the runner-up candidate in most of the primaries. But a vocal minority of the delegates preferred one of America's most well-known televangelists, Pastor Elijah Robinson — a rare occasion in American history when a religious leader was a candidate for such a high-level position. Pastor Robinson had halfheartedly professed to be running for president alongside his usual televangelizing, and although his actual chances of getting on the ticket were very slim, he was a very notorious figure, and his followers were disproportionately vocal. Therefore, Robinson's political platform did have a very profound effect on the ultimate version of the Republican Party platform.

Ultimately, the party chose Governor Faith and Senator Winchester as their candidates for president and vice president, respectively.[11] The Republican Party platform included making Christianity the official national religion; eliminating restrictions on the purchase and possession of firearms; and eliminating Social Security, Medicare, any remnants of the Affordable Care Act (aka Obamacare) and other related social "safety net" programs. The party platform dismissed global warming as a scientific hoax, and encouraged the use of fossil fuels. It also encouraged support for innovative approaches to the extraction of oil from underground, including further expanding the use of hydraulic fracturing, or fracking.[12]

Elections Approach; Viewpoints Diverge

In summary: The Democratic candidates were Henry Castro and Cynthia Wong, campaigning for social justice, tax reform, gun control, environmental preservation, reproductive rights, and equal pay for women. Meanwhile, their Republican opponents, Christine Faith and Henry Winchester, were campaigning for slashing what they called "entitlements" (otherwise known as social "safety net" programs), cutting taxes, deregulating firearms altogether, removing environmental protections, and banning abortions.

The primary elections in 2028 thus resulted in the nominations of two slates of presidential and vice presidential candidates that provided Americans with a clear choice over their future. The two sets of candidates had diametrically opposing views of what was possible, what was desirable and how to get there. The party platforms were so far apart from each other that it seemed difficult to believe they belonged to people living in the same country; difficult to believe that either of these two disparate camps might describe the political

---

11 There were rumors in the media that Pastor Robinson had withdrawn his candidacy in exchange for a Cabinet position.

12 For more about fracking, see the subsection "Environmental Protection and Energy Use" in Appendix 2.

aspirations of one people, with over two hundred years of common heritage and experience. Many political observers felt that the outcome of the 2028 primary elections very much reflected the hyper-polarization of American politics that emerged in 2016 when Hillary Clinton, a Democrat ran against Donald Trump, a Republican. That election was also another case of the winner of popular votes (Clinton), losing the election to the winner of the electoral votes (Trump.) The American people may have had a common heritage, but no longer seemed to share common aspirations. America was no longer one nation, indivisible, with liberty and justice for all.

The Presidential Election: Tuesday Surprise

On November 7, 2028, the first Tuesday in November and therefore Election Day, after years and weeks and months of media frenzy, voters finally got to go to the actual polls, and cast their votes. Despite the completely polarized options, voter turnout proved to be not much different from the country's sinking average: 46.7% of registered voters.[13] As is usual for an American national Election Day, most television and social media feeds were full of nothing but election results, with the United States map on every screen — and the now-ubiquitous symbolic system in place, in which states turned either Red or Blue as the results came in. Political junkies wielded apps that would send smart-device notifications when states turned one color or the other, and so offices, coffee shops, and subway trains on Election Day were full of dings, pings and vibrations.

All that day, some citizens remained glued to their screens into the night, and others tuned out entirely, overwhelmed by the media frenzy and glad that it would — they thought — soon be over. That evening, people went to bed with the full expectation that in the

---

13 Even if 100% of *registered* voters had showed up at the polls, it would still have been only about 70% of the voting-age population.

morning they would know who their president would be, regardless of whether or not they would be pleased with the choice.

But that did not happen!

By late evening — 11:35 p.m. PST — Fox News concluded that the Republican candidate, Texas Governor Christine Faith, had won the election. A few minutes later, at 11:46, MSNBC and CNN concluded that California Senator Henry Castro was the winner. One thing was clear: the election results were too close to call.

On Wednesday morning, the situation was not any clearer than the night before. Several states were still counting absentee ballots, and results were still arriving from rural counties. Florida pre-emptively began a statewide by-hand recount. Speculation ran wild; Fox, MSNBC and CNN all stood by their respective projections, and Twitter and Facebook went crazy. People all over the country posted anecdotal stories of supposed voter fraud, speculations about aliens and the planets' alignment, and numerous other conspiracy theories.

The uncertainty continued all the way until Friday morning, when analysts began to get a clearer picture of the election results. It seemed that this 2028 presidential election had resulted in a situation that had happened very rarely in United States' history — only five times (1876, 1888, 1960, 2000, and 2016): The candidate who received the majority of votes nationwide did not receive the required number of electoral votes (in this case, 270) needed to take office.

Senator Castro and his running mate, Governor Wong, won 53.7% of the popular vote, but received just 268 electoral votes, two shy of the minimum. Governor Faith and her running mate, William Winchester, took 270 electoral votes, the absolute minimum number of votes to assume the presidency. But, they received only 46.3% of the popular vote. It was a technical victory for the Republican presidential candidate. But her victory did not provide the Republican Party with the moral legitimacy to govern 345 million people.

Therefore, we the American people were stuck with two definitions of the "winner": one candidate had won the popular vote, and one had won the electoral vote. The election results did not provide a clear answer as to who had won the election. But it did make one thing clear: The United States of America was politically and morally divided.

Making election results even more questionable were reports of computer problems in calculating the popular votes in several states, including New York, California, Texas and Ohio. Several online publications claimed that a computer problem was caused by North Korean hackers. Or the Chinese. Or the Russians. Others blamed software bugs in the voting machines, or worse still, calculated digital sabotage. Indeed, in cases where the voting system included both a paper ballot and a computerized count, voting inspectors did find anomalies. There was a significant possibility that computer malfunction(s) had affected the election results in a very significant way.

On Friday morning, every online social media site, every blog, the front page of every print newspaper and the first story in every online newspaper in the country, every news program, and every talk show had an opinion about what the real outcome of the election was for America. Some called for nullifying the election results. Others wanted to delay the assuming of office by the new president, regardless of who he or she was. Some called for new elections. Some Southern senators were urging attacking North Korea.

Who would have thought that a country that was known for the high degree of purity in its electoral process[14] could face such a convoluted mess!

That Friday, November 10th, something even more significant happened: quietly, and right before the weekend break, the State of Nevada became the 38th state in the Union to approve the 28th amendment to the United States Constitution, an amendment that

---

14 Relative purity ... see Chicago.

provided for direct presidential election.[15] With Nevada's approval, the amendment had the required ratification of three-fourths of the states. United States would abandon its archaic Electoral College presidential election in favor of directly electing the president and vice president by popular vote.

And with this approval, the presidential election system changed forever!

But ... what was not clear was the effective date of this amendment. It seems this issue had not been made clear in the original congressional bill. No one expected that the passage of the amendment would be so close to a presidential election. Additionally, the results of the 2028 election were not yet officially settled, making it technically still in progress. Would the 28th Amendment apply to the presidential election of 2028? Or would it take effect with the presidential election of 2032?

No one seemed quite sure. Legal scholars were divided. There was indeed real ambiguity in the language of the original legislation. The Democrats were confused. The Republicans were confused. The whole world was confused.

The only people who seemed to know the answer were, predictably, Senator Castro and Governor Faith. Castro (winner of the popular vote) issued an analysis of the law stating that the popular-vote amendment applied to the 2028 election. Faith (winner of the electoral vote) announced that the amendment was clearly not meant to take effect until 2032. Aside from these two individuals and their advisers, no one had a clear and firm answer.

---

15 In 2021, John D. Henry, chairman of the House Judiciary Committee, introduced an amendment to replace the presidential electoral system with one popular vote for president. But after one year of debate, it did clear the House, and was sent to the Senate in the spring of 2023. Despite an attempt by Southern states to filibuster the legislation, the proposed amendment was approved as a joint resolution by Congress in June 2023. The Office of the Federal Register then sent it out to the states for their ratification. For this amendment to go into effect, it needed to be approved by three-fourths of the state legislatures (38 states) by 2029.

The entire country was divided. Conveniently, the division followed a suspiciously partisan line: Democrats were certain that the amendment applied to the presidential election in 2028; Republicans were likewise certain that the amendment was meant to apply to the 2032 election.

Historically, when the country had struggled with fundamental legal and constitutional questions, Washington looked to the United States Supreme Court for answers and clarification. This time was no exception. The Supreme Court did not have to be convinced to take quick action. The chief justice of the Supreme Court, William Spencer, announced on Friday, November 17th, that the court would convene on Monday, November 20th, to hear arguments from the solicitor general as well as from attorneys representing the Republican and Democratic parties. The court was to convene at 9 a.m. sharp.

Over the weekend, law libraries nationwide were filled with attorneys, law clerks and reporters trying to research the issues. As the professionals did their research, the pseudoprofessionals took to the airwaves and the internet to speculate, argue and predict. Every talk show was full of nothing but experts and "experts," arguing about which side would win and which side was right (which was not always the same answer). Many internet portals shut down, overwhelmed by the dramatic increase in traffic. Within hours, bumper stickers and T-shirts were for sale online and in the streets, with slogans advocating for and against both candidates, as well as against the whole process in general: "Don't Blame Me, I Voted for Darth Vader" and the like.

Meanwhile, individual people all over the country, not sure of their impending fate, took to the streets. Many felt compelled to make some sort of statement in support of their own point of view, confusing as it was to arrive at one. Street corners in cities large and small were crowded with small groups of people holding signs professing everything from "Anarchy Now!" to "One Nation, Under God" to "I Never Graduated From Electoral College." In the downtown streets of major cities nationwide, hordes of drone-cars from the service Adverdrivers ® circled and circled, plastered with messages for and against both candidates, and aerial drones of various clever designs zoomed by overhead streaming banners behind them. Vendors also took advantage of the crowds: people hawked T-shirts, hats, umbrellas, fans, blankets, and glow bracelets; food trucks and ice cream sellers made the rounds, and everywhere in the country it was a chaotic and strangely festive weekend. As many would later write, during that uneasy weekend there was a certain electricity all over the country, but no one knew where it was going or what it meant.

In the Courtroom: A Nation Awaits

On Monday, November 20, 2028, at exactly 9 a.m., the Supreme Court convened to hear *Faith v. Castro*. At exactly 11:05 a.m., the world changed forever.

At 9 a.m., the nine Supreme Court justices walked into the court, which was packed with legal scholars, professors, and advocates for Senator Castro and Governor Faith. Outside, gathered on the steps, was a huge throng of journalists; beyond them was a safety barrier set up by police, and beyond the barrier was an enormous crowd stretching for blocks, holding up signs for both parties as well as for unrelated causes. A few miles away, the National Mall was also crammed full of people holding signs, waving flags, or just waiting for the verdict. The mall and surrounding areas were ringed with riot police, though they stood calmly and at ease, and many carried American flags. The mood was both tense and festive; nothing so exciting had happened in American politics in years.

Across the nation, people were glued to their screens: since there was still no recording of any kind allowed inside the Supreme Court, the closest that cameras could get was the steps outside. Everyone inside had to pass through a detector and check their personal devices with security at the door, to prevent anyone from illegally recording the proceedings.

Inside the courtroom, according to court transcripts, the solicitor general was the first person to speak to the justices, followed by the general counsel for the National Democratic Party, followed by her Republican counterpart. Opening remarks progressed as normal.

At 11:05 a.m., attendees became aware of a loud and strange noise, like the roar of a distant oncoming train. Lights flickered off and the sound system went silent, cutting off the Republican counsel's opening remarks midsentence. Then, in the blink of an eye, as the stunned and frightened attendees witnessed in horror, the floor moved with a violent jerk. The ceiling collapsed. People screamed. The walls came down. Everything went dark.

As first responders rushed to the scene, people across the nation were confused, frightened, and angry, as live feeds from the courthouse steps went black — and did not come back up. Major social media sites were almost instantly flooded with panicked posts. Faced only with the dead news feed, people immediately blamed everyone from the government to the TV networks to Russia to North Korea to China to Mideast terrorism. After just one minute of no video feed, people were already asking each other, "Who should we attack?!"

Meanwhile, many who were close enough to be eyewitnesses to the destructive event were uploading comments, selfies, and short videos of the situation: shaky snippets of fleeing crowds, selfies of people with cuts and bruises, descriptions of screams and flying rubble, all fueled the hasty conclusions of a panicking nation.

What no one outside the walls knew was: what was happening inside the Supreme Court? And who, or what, was responsible?

It wasn't until 11:25 a.m. that CNN managed to begin broadcasting again live from the actual scene outside the court building. Its small self-digging robot "CDPC" (for CNN Disaster Probe Camera) had managed to literally dig its way into the collapsed building of the Supreme Court, and provide some images from inside. As the feed came back up, CNN was quick to tout this unique capability, "by now standard on all CNN news vans," and "first of its kind for any news media" imagery, before handing off to the news crew that were on the scene.

Reporter Brianna Patel, looking into the camera with the dazed look of one who has just been pushed out of an airplane without a parachute, began describing the devastation around her. Speaking mostly to fill the stunned silence, she described her experience of what had just occurred: the sound, the shaking, the rubble around her, stammering that "it may have been due to an act of terror, an enemy strike, or ... who knows, some sort of crazy seismic event ... right here in the nation's capital."

After a few minutes, an update arrived via her earpiece: there had indeed been a massive earthquake. According to initial U.S.G.S.[16] data, the temblor's strength was estimated at 6.2 on the Richter scale. Patel reported that the specific cause of the earthquake was still unclear, since there was no known major seismic fault near the nation's capital.

Outside the Supreme Court building, the damage elsewhere was also considerable. The National Mall was strewn with rubble, as well as garbage, detritus, and stunned or injured people from the crowds who panicked and ran. Abandoned protest signs lay everywhere, complicating initial damage assessments. The Washington Monument, essentially just a rigid concrete pillar, was severely cracked. At the Library of Congress, numerous librarians would later be discovered trapped in the stacks, penned in among piles of books hurled from shelves. National treasures in the archives at the Smithsonian and other surrounding museums were bruised, broken, and thrown across the room. The Capitol sustained serious damage: its iconic dome was renovated in 2016, but years of rusting and seepage rendered brittle the underlying structure, and it fractured in half like a broken egg

16 United States Geological Survey — which now belongs to the American Republic of Compassion and is referred to as the ARC Geological Survey.

and crashed to earth. Luckily for the congresspeople, most of them had taken an early lunch, and most of the staffers had taken the opportunity to play hooky, given the unusual circumstances of the day, so the dome missed hitting anyone as it came down.

As for the White House, that residence was secured against a nuclear blast, so apart from a few dishes and vases falling here and there, everyone inside was fine — including a few tour groups who would all go on to sign book deals about their experience that began that day with a few brief, tense hours on lockdown inside the presidential residence.

At 1 p.m. on the day of the earthquake, Fox News showed the coverage of the devastation at the Supreme Court and the surrounding areas. Its anchor, Jim O'Shaughnessy, who was already in town covering the historic court battle, interviewed terrorism expert Jack Stalkins at the Heritage Foundation (also very close to the epicenter, located less than half a mile to the north) who declared, staring straight into the camera, "The destruction of the Supreme Court must be the work of Muslim terrorists." When Mr. Stalkins was reminded of the earlier USGS diagnosis that pointed to an earthquake being the cause of the disaster, he remained undaunted, insisting that a terroristinduced explosion could have unleashed an earthquake as well.

Mr. O'Shaughnessy commented[17] that some members of Congress were advocating bombing Indonesia in retaliation. There was no discussion of why Indonesia, except that Indonesia's population of 290 million consisted primarily of Muslims.

Later that day, CNN switched to the West Coast, where local reporter Aaron Guzman was inside the office of Dr. Beverly Ghosh, chair of the Department of Geology at Caltech. Looking into the camera and seeming more than a little rattled, Dr. Ghosh gave her explanation: "At this time, we geologists believe hydraulic fracturing, known informally as "fracking," in areas near Philadelphia during the

17 Unfounded, since he had not had a chance to speak with any members of Congress at all in the previous two hours.

past several years has reactivated a long-dormant seismic fault — or conceivably created a new one — through parts of Pennsylvania and Maryland, in the Marcellus Shale, one of the largest shale gas deposits in the nation. As I testified before Congress a few years ago, there are several precedents for this type of human-induced earthquake, and that tremors in unusual places, probably induced by fracking, have been observed as early as 2012. I believe that the new fault runs, essentially, directly under the Supreme Court, and it was that which caused the earthquake."

Then she stared straight at the lens. "I tried to warn Congressman Cannon and the Science Subcommittee what science was telling us, in fact, *warning* us, about the potential for fracking-induced earthquakes, but it wasn't what they wanted to hear."[18]

Rescue workers and reporters spent hours all over the wreckage of the National Mall and the government buildings. As in any disaster, reports of the damage and the death toll varied enormously. By the end of the day, it was confirmed by first responders and area hospitals that the earthquake had caused 46 deaths and 900 injuries, including seven members of the U.S. Supreme Court, who were severely injured and remained in a comatose state.

---

18 For more about Dr. Ghosh's earlier testimony, see Appendix 2.

CHAPTER TWO

The Great Separation

WITH SEVEN OF NINE SUPREME Court Justices incapacitated, the results of the presidential election *still* undecided, and a nation on the verge of panic, one thing was clear; whatever happened next should happen quickly.

For two weeks, each media outlet whipped its own demographic into an appropriate frenzy. The earthquake in Washington D.C. and its timing gave rise to rumors about a possible governmental, military, immigrant, gay, feminist, or extraterrestrial conspiracy. Some pundits called for a military coup to restore trust and order. Anarchists wondered whether now would be the time for an uprising. Abroad, the incident was portrayed mostly in editorial cartoons: a bald eagle with its eggs broken; a Statue of Liberty sopping wet after tripping and falling into the sea; the Founding Fathers ripping up the Constitution and throwing the pieces into the air, etc. Meanwhile, at home, day-to-day nonessential government operations ground to a halt: schools were closed and all court cases postponed. Militia groups, homeless shelters, schools, police departments, city governments, and communists began making logistical plans to combat societal chaos. (According to aides, the incumbent president, Ray Ryan, was holed up in an undisclosed location and was purportedly "staying out of it.") Amazingly, widespread chaos did not in fact ensue.

Instead, the two disputed leaders of the country made an unprecedented announcement, to create a new kind of trust and order. On Thursday, December 7th, at a ceremony at Arlington National Cemetery coinciding with the 87th anniversary of the Japanese attack on Pearl Harbor, Senator Castro and Governor Faith issued a joint statement to the press.[1]

In front of an immense throng bristling with thrusting cameras and microphones, they announced that they had reached an agreement: on a temporary basis, and until further notice, they would share the presidency.

They stood close together, sporting matching flag lapel pins. They smiled, and spoke in measured voices as they amicably took turns. From the script released to the press:

CASTRO:

I'm sure you're all aware of the ambiguity surrounding the effective date of the 28th Amendment to the Constitution. This means that the imbalance between the popular vote and the Electoral College results makes it unclear just who ought to be president of the United States.

---

1 The incumbent president, Ray Ryan, was there too; he stood in the background in silence and mopped his brow repeatedly with a white handkerchief. In the years since President Ryan was first elected, the government had gotten so contentious that he ended up taking more vacation days than workdays in a single year, and was in the news even less often than his own vice president. Press analysts read his silence and the white handkerchief as, consciously or subconsciously, a signal of surrender.

FAITH:

Additionally, there's some question about how accurate the vote even is. Voter fraud, alleged hacking by North Koreans and possibly other bad actors internationally, makes it almost impossible to determine whether the election results are truly accurate in the first place.

CASTRO:

Regardless, this dilemma speaks to the deep political divides in American society today.

FAITH:

America is more polarized than heads versus tails, right now.

CASTRO:

Both myself and Governor Faith adhere to the principles that government should be held responsible by the people whom it governs.

FAITH:

And I agree with Senator Castro that he and I have a duty to answer to the people, since we are a government of the people, by the people, and for the people.

CASTRO:

So we and our political advisers and lawyers have come to a momentous and bold decision.

FAITH:

We are going to go down in history as a couple of mavericks.

[Laughter from both]

CASTRO:

If we may supersede the question of the 28th Amendment, which the very political polarization itself renders impossible to solve ...

FAITH:

... We have agreed that I, Christine Faith, will represent the states in which I received the majority of the popular vote ...

CASTRO:

... and I, Henry Castro, will represent the states in which I received a majority of the popular vote.

TOGETHER:

We will share the presidency.

After that statement came a cacophony of applause, screaming, wailing, shouted questions and other vocal chaos. The uproar lasted a full five minutes.

American democracy did, it seem, survive the voting disaster and the collapse of the Supreme Court.

At each subsequent meeting and press conference, the candidates stressed that this sharing of the presidency, each heading up their own group of states, was a temporary arrangement. They both agreed that within a reasonable time period, they would call a national convention to address the issues that had created the confusion. Until then, however, each would serve as the elected president of a sovereign nation, referred to temporarily as "The United Blue States" and "The United Red States." Because of the national confusion, they each considered their governments to be provisionally in operation already, instead of waiting for the lame-duck period of the previous term to be over.[2]

There was no threat of military confrontation; no national uprising; no mass demonstrations. No burning of buildings; no assassinations. The "American spring" was a peaceful one. We had now become the "Un-tied" States of America.

Conquering and Dividing: Ex Uno Plures

This new double-nation creation was in line with the emerging tone of the U.S. Constitution, which now, with the passage of the 28th Amendment, provided for direct election of the president via popular vote. Further, the legislative branches flanking each new Executive Branch would consist of the representatives of the states that had voted for that respective president. Given this broad and rather logical division, they needed to agree on the states in which each candidate had received the majority of the votes. Based upon the

2   The incumbent president, Ray Ryan, gratefully took this opportunity to silently retire; he and his family moved back to Florida to run an alligator ranch and bask in the sunshine.

existing results, the states in the table below became part of Senator Castro's republic, known at this point in history as the "United Blue States":

States Won by Castro: "United Blue States"		
California	Massachusetts	Oregon
Colorado	Michigan	Pennsylvania
Connecticut	Minnesota	Rhode Island
Delaware	Nevada	Vermont
Hawaii	New Jersey	Virginia
Illinois	New Mexico	Washington
Maryland	New York	Wisconsin

Governor Faith's portfolio, the "United Red States," included the states listed in the table below:

States Won by Faith: "United Red States"		
Alabama	Kansas	North Dakota
Alaska	Kentucky	Ohio
Arizona	Louisiana	Oklahoma
Arkansas	Maine	South Carolina
Florida	Mississippi	South Dakota
Georgia	Missouri	Tennessee
Idaho	Montana	Texas
Indiana	Nebraska	Utah
Iowa	New Hampshire	West Virginia
	North Carolina	Wyoming

As one can see from the inset map, this arrangement, formalized in this way, definitely presented some logistical problems. While the United Red States were largely contiguous, with the exception of Alaska and the Northeast enclave of New Hampshire/Maine, the

MAP OF 2028 U.S. PRESIDENTIAL ELECTION RESULTS:

(WHICH LED TO THE SUBSEQUENT DIVISION OF THE COUNTRY INTO
THE UNITED RED STATES AND THE UNITED BLUE STATES)

FAITH (R) - UNITED RED STATES:

CASTRO (D) - UNITED BLUE STATES:

United Blue States were separated into islands. There was the entire West Coast, a Rocky Mountain duet, a Great Lakes zone, and most of New England. Then there was Hawaii, which had always been both noncontiguous with the mainland, and itself made up of unconnected islands. Jokes abounded in the Hawaiian media about how finally the rest of their country knows exactly how they've always felt.

Analysts were quick to point out that this was not completely unprecedented in world history, as there are two countries that exist entirely landlocked within the larger country of South Africa, and there are also parts of the border between India and Pakistan where islands of one country's land exist completely inside the other country's boundaries. It seemed indisputable, however, that this particular patchwork entanglement of countries had never existed before on such a large geographical scale.

The people were reassured that any logistical problems that were sure to arise from this arrangement would be dealt with when they came up. In the meantime, citizens and analysts alike were left to stare at the red-and-blue map, and be reminded perhaps of Ben Franklin's divided snake flag that read, "JOIN, or DIE."[3]

---

3   Thomas, Allen C, *A history of Pennsylvania* (1913). p. 117

CHAPTER THREE

What Happened Here?

"Remember, democracy never lasts long. It soon wastes, exhausts, and murders itself."

- John Adams

"America will never be destroyed from the outside. If we falter and lose our freedoms, it will be because we destroyed ourselves."

- Abraham Lincoln

Creating One Country: E Pluribus Unum

At this point, which marks perhaps the end of the United States, I wish to briefly examine its beginning, and the precarious nature of its existence — it reminds this author of a historical palindrome.[1]

---

1   Author's note: I had prepared what was, in my mind, an incredibly well-researched and thoughtful examination of the history of the Decline and Fall of the United States … but my editor insisted that it was "too long" for the "short attention spans" of the "current

The United States was created from disparate pieces and remained together, through numerous wars, before disintegrating again into component parts. Given the ideological differences that caused the Separation, is it not ironic that the event which ultimately brought the union to its (temporary?) end was an act of either God or Science — depending on which universal force one places one's faith?

The United States had perhaps as messy and confusing a creation as it did a separation, and almost never existed in the first place. The government as we knew it came from thirteen separate colonies, all founded by the British crown. How did these thirteen separate colonies, evolving separately and founded over the course of 125 years, become one Union in the first place? Britain imposed a series of taxes upon the colonists, which inspired the colonists to rebel, beginning what would become the American Revolutionary War. Their political response, the First Continental Congress, a meeting of delegates from all the colonies (except Georgia) was the first time that the colonies had banded together to act as one political unit.

In fact, history almost took the colonies in a very different direction; if earlier in 1754 a smaller Albany Congress had adopted Ben Franklin's "Plan of Union," we might have turned out not unlike Canada, our neighbor to the north:

> *"The plan was considered very attractive to most of the members, as it proposed a popularly elected Grand Council which would represent the interests of the colonies as a whole, and would be a continental equivalent to the English Parliament. Poised against this would be a President General, appointed by the crown, to represent the authority of the king in America."* [2]

---

generation," and that I should "get to the g-ddamned earthquake." After a brief argument in which a certain number of wine bottles may or may not have been thrown across the room and one or more of the room's occupants may have been caused to bleed, we came to an intellectual compromise and rearranged the chapters. My thoughtful treatise may be found in the back of this book, in Appendix 2 ("A Country Divided").

2   Plan of Union

The United States might have continued on as part of the British Commonwealth, and the First Continental Congress[3] in 1774 voted on the Galloway Plan, an updated version of Franklin's Plan of Union — but thanks to Boston's outright defiance of the "Intolerable Acts," radicals persuaded the Congress to reject the Galloway Plan — by a very narrow margin.

By 1776, political opinion and public support (whipped up by publications such as Thomas Paine's treatise *Common Sense*) pushed the Second Continental Congress to formally declare the independence of the United States of America, famously finalizing the document and signing it on July 4, 1776 — in the middle of a week when the British fleet was arriving to invade.

Also signed during warfare were the Articles of Confederation, formally declaring the United States of America as a political entity in "Perpetual Union," and outlining the ramifications and practicalities of that union: Article II states: "Each state retains its sovereignty, freedom, and independence, and every Power, Jurisdiction and right, which is not by this confederation expressly delegated to the United States, in Congress assembled." In other words, the states had become unified — but only just.

After the Revolutionary War officially ended in 1783, there was a bit more leisure time to figure out what this new country was going to look like … it wasn't until four years later that the Constitution replaced the looser central government set up by the Articles of Confederation. To be sure, the Founding Fathers did disagree with each other about the role of government and appropriate structures to ensure the development of what they deemed important societal values. But in the end, they were somehow able to reach agreement, and together they drafted a constitution that remained the country's fundamental governing document for over 200 years.

---

3   Presumably it was just called the Continental Congress before there was another one.

The Country that Stays Together, Stays Together

Before the Great Separation, the only previous major threat to the union came almost 100 years after its birth, when the country fought a major civil war over the issue of slavery — a war that resulted in approximately 625,000 deaths, and higher by some estimates. More Americans died during that conflict than were killed in every single war that came after it — combined. The American Civil War came very close to tearing the republic in two. But at the end, through the leadership of President Abraham Lincoln, the Union states prevailed over the Confederacy, and the country remained structurally, if not spiritually, united.

After the Civil War, the United States of America remained united for almost 150 more years. This union persisted despite many further trials, including a severe economic depression that almost destroyed the very foundation of American society and its capitalist economic structure in the late 1920s. Even American participation in two world wars did not significantly damage the functional political unity of the American people, measuring by the will of the voting public:[4] President Franklin D. Roosevelt was elected to office in four landslide elections, spanning the two world wars.[5] It appears that, throughout the mid-twentieth century, there was a significant voting majority who, whether or not they agreed on the fundamental issues of the time, were able to reach consensus in resolving them.

Cracks Appear

Beginning with the early 1960s, however, against the backdrop of the war in Vietnam and the resulting deaths of more than 50,000 Americans, citizens of the United States began to publicly question

---

4   Which by WWII happily was a more accurate representation of the population, since the voting population by then included women as well as African Americans.

5   FDR remained in office from 1933 until his sudden death on March 29, 1945. The 22nd Amendment to the Constitution, passed in 1947 and finally ratified by three-fourths of the states in 1951, thereafter — for good or ill — limited any president to two terms.

their fundamental assumptions regarding race, environment, personal freedom, and the role and extent of government. The 1960s brought an onslaught of overlapping public protest movements: the protests against the Vietnam War; the "counterculture" protests against conservatism and general social conformity; the sexual revolution; the Civil Rights movement; the Hispanic and Chicano movement; the feminist movement; and the gay/LGBTQ rights movement. One could argue that during the 1960s America experienced a bloodless social revolution that undermined what had hitherto been, at least on its face, a societal consensus. To quote a Pre-Separation blog entry, "Some called this era [the 1960s] a classical Jungian nightmare cycle, where a rigid culture, unable to contain the demands for greater individual freedom, broke free of the social constraints of the previous age through extreme deviation from the norm."[6]

Cracks Widen

Although the social revolution(s) began in the early 1960s, it wasn't until the presidency of Richard Nixon that America's ability to uphold outward social consensus truly began its final descent. Nixon, a Republican, won the 1968 presidential election in a stormy election season: The North Vietnamese People's Army and the Viet Cong launched the Tet Offensive against American troops, President Lyndon B. Johnson withdrew his candidacy for a second term, and Senator Robert F. Kennedy was assassinated. The election results were close, with Nixon winning 301 electoral votes — just 31 more than the 270 needed to win. In his victory speech, he coined the slogan "Bring Us Together"

A nation weary of turmoil may indeed have embraced that sentiment, for Nixon went on to be reelected in 1972 with a landslide

---

6   https://shuhuifyp.wordpress.com/2009/08/03/socio-political-climate-of-1960s/

victory.[7] However, Nixon also went on to resign the presidency amid the Watergate scandal in 1974. It is fair to say, given subsequent events, that he did not succeed in Bringing Us Together, after all.

This unprecedented event — the actual resignation of a president — may indeed have triggered widespread disillusionment in the idea of American unity. After 1974, election results began to oscillate wildly, alternating between extremely close calls and landslide victories. In the 1980 election, President Jimmy Carter won by a very narrow margin: 297 electoral votes to Gerald Ford's 240. In 1984, President Ronald Reagan (who, it must be said, was an ex-movie actor and therefore used to winning the hearts of the populace) won, with a landslide never again equaled or surpassed: Reagan won 525 electoral votes; Walter Mondale received just 13, taking only Minnesota and the District of Columbia.

Though he had been elected by a landslide, Reagan's subsequent presidency contributed to the growing ideological division, driving public policy sharply to the right. Reagan slashed social programs and exponentially increased defense spending — yet because his presidency coincided with an upswing from a recession in the late 1970s, the gradual improvement of the economy obscured the full impact of his ideological actions.

Meanwhile, another movement was helping to publicly pull the country in different directions: as another result of the activist movements of the 1960s, minorities were busy making inroads into the political sphere. Lots of candidates were becoming very public "firsts": Shirley Chisholm, Patsy Mink, Geraldine Ferraro, Jesse Jackson. Opinions and experiences that were different than America's usual political mainstream were thus gaining visibility — and when these minority candidates lost their elections, perhaps that visibility added fuel to the fire under those who supported them.

---

7   Nixon won 520 electoral votes versus George McGovern's 17. He carried every single state but Massachusetts and the District of Columbia.

Mind the Gap: Money and Media in the Information Age

The arrival of a postindustrial society, brought about by the evolution of information technology, fundamentally changed the nature of the American economic system, including the composition and the size of American social classes.

Thanks to economic policy, the middle class steadily shrank over the years, from 61% of the population in 1971 to just 31% of the population in 2021. America was thus becoming polarized not just politically, but socioeconomically, becoming a land of the super-rich and the super-poor.

Along with more money came more (and more disproportionate) influence in politics. In 2010, a decision by the U.S. Supreme Court, known as "Citizens United," allowed corporations and labor unions to spend unlimited amounts of money in support of (or against) political candidates — by spending money indirectly on political tools, rather than on campaigns directly. With virtually unlimited and anonymous financial support from corporations and wealthy individuals, candidates in federal elections no longer had to be so concerned with garnering the support of the general public.

Cultural divisions, combined with economic stratification, contributed to the country's polarization. The two parties, rather than try to find compromises on each other's favored issues, mostly pressed on ahead in opposite directions, pursuing their own agenda while denigrating the other party's.

Concentrating and magnifying both the economic gap and the diverging political agendas was the rise of the internet and social media. Where before, say, 1996, people had to work hard to find information and opinions that were not readily available in the mainstream media, after the internet became widespread, people from all across the country could easily find people who shared their interests, and read only news and opinions that bolstered and echoed their own views.

The proliferation of mass media sources in the United States took advantage of this trend and contributed to the accelerated separation of Blue-state and Red-state zeitgeist, by providing "flavored" news, and even fake news, tailor-made to fit the interests of their target demographics. The U.S. public quickly adapted to viewing and listening to news that bolstered their own preconceptions. The resulting splitting of the U.S. audience into two distinct points of view, each with its own custom news outlets, accelerated the trend of each side only hearing news that reinforced its own opinions.

The hyper-polarization of the country was evident, particularly after the 2016 general elections, when Donald Trump, a Republican, won enough electoral college votes to defeat Democrat Hillary Clinton for U.S. presidency, even though she clearly won the popular vote. The chain of events (including Russia's involvement, in favor of Trump) further solidified the political divide, leading many to view 2016 as the true beginning of the Great Separation, that took place in 2029.

George Orwell's novel *1984* defines the concept of "doublethink" as "the power of holding two contradictory beliefs in one's mind simultaneously, and accepting both of them." If the United States may be said to be a metaphorical single mind, that mind was becoming adept at doublethink — but instead of two contradictory beliefs, it contained two sets of people with contradictory beliefs. The strong factions who held beliefs opposite their rivals also did not have to interact or agree with their rivals very much; the United States was becoming something of a split personality that couldn't split.

That is, until the Great Earthquake, and then the Great Separation.

CHAPTER FOUR

Two New Countries?

Creating Two Countries - Un-tying the States

With two effectively separate governments Post-Separation, (save that they each kept the United States Constitution as their foundational text), the two "temporary" presidents were essentially heads of state for two entirely new countries. Each new country was like a mini-United States: a group of states with their own government, but united under a federal government. Each of these countries would need a new name if it wanted to distinguish itself as a distinct identity. "The United Blue States" and "The United Red States" were all right for the interim, but they had been selected with the understanding that another name would be found. Neither president wanted his or her country to be the last to come up with a name, so their administrations each promptly got to work setting up their own polls.

Henry Castro asked Gallup to conduct a poll to determine what his country's citizens would like the country to be known by.

It was a frantic few weeks for Gallup, since they had to redo their algorithms to create a representative sample of just the population and demographics of the Blue states in question, rather than the entirety of the United States. Adding to their woes was the fact that residents in Blue states were more likely to exclusively use cell phones or other private numbers, and also to be less likely to answer telemarketing calls. They resorted to heavier use of some newer polling strategies, such as survey-ads before websites and online videos.

After the polling process was finally complete, 56% of the people in Castro's republic opted for the temporary name "Republic of Compassion." That name received a boost from the fact that several weeks earlier, the host of a popular TV comedy program (Comedy Central's *The Daily Show*, now the most reliable source of accurate news in the country) had referred to Henry Castro as "president of the American Republic of Compassion." Castro agreed that his legislative branch would decide on the final name when it convened in January of the following year.

Christine Faith, meanwhile, decided to take advantage of Fox Network's offer to conduct a national poll to determine a name for her country. Fox already had detailed demographic information on the makeup of Red states, and personal information on millions of individuals, so their process was speedier. After a week of polling, the Fox Network announced that the citizens of the new country had decided on a name representative of the predominant Red state culture. Over 67% of the people chose as the name of their new country: The Armed Christian Nations of America.

United States of Diaspora: The Great Migrations

The two leaders acknowledged that, while this division of the United States was surely temporary, it would result in many people being suddenly assigned to a country that did not completely represent their political ideology. After all, some states, such as Ohio and

New Hampshire, were more "purple" than others. This geographic dislocation, the presidents-elect both agreed, would be a problem. But then they came up with a creative solution. Any individual who felt that he or she was in the wrong country would have six months to relocate to the other country without having to declare a change of citizenship. Each government offered to provide help with relocation, including financial assistance and reduced-rate or free transportation and moving services. To ensure that such individuals would choose the right country for them, a joint committee of the American Republic of Compassion (ARC) and the Armed Christian Nations of America (ACNA) met for two weeks and developed a survey, officially entitled "Country Relocation Algorithm," but popularly referred to as "What's the Color of Your Soul?" survey, to assist with the voluntary relocation. Residents could complete the survey online.[1] (See Appendix 1 to view or take the survey.)

Individuals who scored 80 or higher automatically would become citizens of the ACNA; people who scored 40 or below would become citizens of the ARC. These two groups would be given financial assistance to relocate to the appropriate country. Individuals who scored between 40 and 80 had one year to decide which country in which to declare citizenship, but these individuals would not receive any financial assistance for relocation. Since taking one whole year to choose would void the chance of financial assistance, this policy prompted the vast majority of centrists and independents to choose a side, and quickly.[2] By the time of this writing — virtually at the one-year mark — there are very few cross-border moves taking place anymore.

---

1   Residents of Washington, D.C. and U.S. territories would also be allowed to take part in the process.

2   There are already online communities popping up consisting of people calling them-selves the Independent Diaspora. Many commenters therein are urging Independents to move to Canada — though independents have been threatening that for years, and so far there has never yet been proven a great migration to the north. Some groups advocate buying mobile homes, and joining America's Romany communities.

The relocation process was made easier by both grassroots and entrepreneurial efforts to facilitate processes like house-swapping. RedForBlue.com and CountrySwap.com were the two busiest commercial real-estate sites: there, you could see the average value of your own home and search for homes in the other country of the same approximate value, and even in a neighborhood analogous to your current one. Or, if you wished, you could search for something different from what you already had, comparing cities, prices and home styles. Some people chose to trade, full-out; others were betting that this arrangement wouldn't last, and they opted for long-term home swaps.

Citizens of both countries also made heavy use of Craigslist and other freecycle-type sites, which offered more even-trade and sharing options. Through these home-swapping sites and through social media, people who had not known each other before the Separation organized themselves into large caravans for the moving process, and it was common to see long lines of cars and vans with banners driving cross-country. Sometimes a particular caravan might stretch for more than a mile. It was a festive time, since caravaners often drove with their windows down, playing music, singing, playfully mooning each other, snapping pictures and selfies, and stopping in large groups to eat and stretch their legs. Late 2028 and early 2029 was quite a boom time for rural towns and roadside diners, which had been experiencing ever more difficult economic conditions in the 21st century. Diners and restaurants would even put up red or blue flags in their windows or along the highways near exits, to signal accommodations and fellow feeling.[3]

The color purple is still seen as a fashion faux pas, in both countries. Internationally, however, in 2029 purple is having a major fashion moment.

---

3   As the more cynically minded no doubt can guess, many such establishments had two sets of flags, and an efficient highway-monitoring strategy.

Two Capitals: Diverging Mindsets

With the populace already sorting itself into the two countries, the twin administrations turned to symbolic and governmental matters. Presidents Faith and Castro each had to decide where to locate the capitals of their respective countries. Especially given that the formerly united nation's capital was literally in ruins, it seemed both logistically and symbolically important to select new locations for these two new governments.

Governor Faith decided that she was fed up with the Eastern establishment, its socialist ideology and the "beltway bandits." She felt that her presidency would be serving God-fearing Americans and thus she decided that her capital should be located in the Bible Belt. She selected Dallas, Texas, at least on a temporary basis. A major reason for this was that Governor Faith was offered, and accepted, a 20-story office building belonging to the estate of businessman and former independent presidential candidate H. Ross Perot, a building that had been largely vacant for a few years.[4]

Senator Castro was also unhappy about the political climate in Washington, D.C. — and the literal climate as well. With global warming in full swing, the District of Columbia was returning to the swamp from whence it came. He decided that San Francisco, where he had lived and worked for many years, would be the seat of his government. Additionally, he announced that he would move his office to Alcatraz Island, which had a rich and storied history since its discovery in 1775. The island had been a pelican colony, a Mexican military facility, a lighthouse, an American military base, the San Francisco Arsenal, a Civil War prison, and a federal penitentiary. When the military facilities closed in 1963 (shortly after a famous escape), the island became a tourist destination and even occasionally a theater and art venue — and for 19 months the seat of a Native

---

4   The building happened to be located across the street from the Perot Museum of Nature and Science, which was problematic for some of Faith's Cabinet members.

American protest. Its diverse history — and the fact that it was already public land — made it a perfect logistical and symbolic capital.

Each of the new presidents-elect held a solo press conference on Monday, December 4th. Both spoke with their vice president standing closely by. Each president-elect was framed for the camera in front of a representative view of their new capital: President Castro and Vice President Wong stood outside one of the historic buildings on Alcatraz Island, with a view of the ocean and misty San Francisco behind them. President Faith and Vice President Winchester stood on the roof of their new office building, in front of the downtown Dallas skyline. The text was prepared jointly ahead of time, by the presidents-elect and their staffs. A portion of each press conference was designed to report information in common, and a portion was for each new executive to describe their platform for their new republic.

The in-common part of the announcement (from the original teleprompter scripts) went as follows:

[FAITH OR CASTRO]:

Greetings, fellow Americans. [Insert name of counterpart] and I have come to an agreement about the next phase of our respective governments, and it's time to formally share the results of that decision with our people.

I'm speaking to you now from the new capital building of the [American Republic of Compassion/Armed Christian Nations of America]. I'm here in beautiful [San Francisco/Dallas,] and [Name of Counterpart] is in beautiful [Dallas/San Francisco]. That's right: we've each selected our capitals, and our families have already moved in. Right now they're probably doing what they always do when we move into a new place: argue about who's got the better room. [Pause for laughter.]

You're probably wondering how this two-capitals situation is going to work. Well, we've decided the legislatures of each country will be made up of the members of Congress from the states that voted for us — the states that are now part of our new nation. Look at your screen now to see a list of those states, or visit our website for details later.

That's two of the three branches of government taken care of: Executive and Legislative; what about the third? I'm sure you've seen by now the footage of what happened in the Supreme Court on that infamous day. Because of the ruin of that judicial body and its questionable legitimacy, we presidents-elect have agreed to appoint our own entirely new Supreme Courts, made up of nine members each. We will each be advised by a member of the old Supreme Court: [I/My counterpart] will be advised by Justice James Propert, and [My counterpart/I] will be advised by Justice Catherine Kaginmore. As they both remain bright and sharp, we're confident they will be glad to help us with this process, before welcoming retirement. Our Supreme Courts will also be located in our new capitals … and thus two new governments, springing from the old deadlocked government, will be born.

Thus, each new president was careful to reassure his or her people about the continuation of a safe, familiar style of government: both outlined their Executive Branch, obliquely mentioning their families in order to give a sense of the homey part of the White House about the new government; they described their Legislative Branch, relieving concern about states still having representation; and they mentioned the start of the new Judicial Branch, which conveniently contained a seed from the old government.

And now, as they continued, they diverged wildly from the safe and familiar and entered electrifying new territory. Each embarked on their own continuation of the shared speech, promising therein to bring to fruition some long-held dreams of their own respective party:

And now, to address the legislative priorities of our own brave new government: …"

Governor Faith's speech continued as follows, mixing her trademark folksy style with some Christian-inspired straight talk:

FAITH (CONT.):

I have a simple set of priorities, y'all, and it boils down to taxes, taxes, and taxes. I'm gonna make our tax system the way we've always wanted it. [Pause for cheering.] First, I'm gonna introduce legislation to eliminate corporate income tax. Companies are always fleeing to the location with the least amount of corporate income tax, leading to loss of jobs and very little revenue for our states anyway. This way, they can stay right where they are, continuing to create jobs and contribute to our economy.

Next, I'm gonna propose a ten percent flat tax for all the citizens of these Armed Christian Nations of America. No matter what you make, everyone pays ten percent. Ten percent! Ten percent is even in the Bible: Genesis 28:22 says, 'And of all that you give me I will give a full tenth to you.' Ten percent from everyone, no matter who you are: it's easy to remember, it's fair, and it's the Christian thing to do.

The third priority is about taxes, but it's also about your safety, and your rights. I'm gonna provide further tax incentives for those states that have 'Stand-Your-Ground' legislation. I know a lot of our states

already have these laws, but I'm gonna make
sure they stay put: all our citizens in the
Armed Christian Nations of America deserve
to exercise their rights to protect their
homes, their families, and their property
from all kinds of attacks.

Together, we can build a wondrous future,
in our new country. Won't you join me, and
help make the Armed Christian Nations of
America the best country on Earth?"

Faith's three top legislative priorities would, if actually fulfilled,
make some long-held Republican dreams come true: no corporate
taxes, a biblically inspired 10% flat tax for citizens, and the rights of
self-defense, with a bonus extra tax cut for states.

In Castro's part of the speech, he spoke about many of the same
issues, but taking the complete opposite path:

CASTRO (CONT.):
Our legislative priorities, going forward,
are simple. In starting anew, we have the
chance to do things right this time. My
first priority is the safety and welfare
of all our citizens. Therefore, I make this
promise to you now: our administration will
not, I repeat, will not have a Defense
Department. The era of world war is over.

In 2026, the United States military budget
was almost half of the entire federal budget.

That's right ... half. And what did this almost half of our budget go to? Much of it went to stockpiling weapons and equipment that we're never going to use, in order to make ourselves seem more dangerous than ever to other countries that we're never going to go to war with. By cutting all defense spending, I can cut taxes for us all, especially the poorest and neediest of our citizens, and still reduce our overall budget by thirty percent.

In the second step toward fostering compassion for all our citizens, it's time to close the wealth gap. Therefore, I propose to limit personal wealth to one hundred million dollars per individual. I think that's enough to live on, don't you? [Pause for laughter.]

Each person will be allowed to amass up to one hundred million dollars worth of cash, investments, properties, and other assets. Above that ceiling, they can do anything they like with their income — except keep it. Imagine: a country where philanthropy becomes a natural sport. 'O brave new world, that has such people in't.' Just think what amazing new heights we might reach as a society, with all that extra money going toward things that will improve the general welfare? Schools, libraries, and public buildings? Educational programs, food banks, scientific research? We could continue to cure cancer, explore space, and figure out how to reverse or slow climate change. As Eleanor Roosevelt once said, 'The future belongs to those who believe in the beauty of their dreams,' and that sounds like a pretty beautiful dream to me.

Another kind of lasting change I'm seeking is the way our politicians are elected. Money has been the driving force behind politics for too long. [Pause for applause.] In the future American Republic of Compassion, political campaigns will be funded by the government. I don't want to abolish political contributions altogether, because I think it's important for citizens to be able to speak out in support of politicians in whom they believe. Therefore, I'm going to allow private — and that includes corporate — campaign donations, but I'm going to reduce the legal limit.

Not two thousand dollars.

Not two hundred.

Not even one hundred.

But one dollar.

One single dollar bill. One dollar is enough to put your support behind someone. If you want to donate more, volunteer your time and your talents … but let's keep money out of politics. [Pause for cheering.]

My third and perhaps most controversial priority is the physical safety of our citizens. As we all have seen, guns and gun violence in the United States was becoming completely insane. Did you know that the United States, as of two years ago, had 150 guns for every 100 people? Is it any wonder, therefore, that the rate of firearm deaths per year in the United States was four times that of the next industrialized nation? And which communities are affected most by these gun deaths? The people who are already historically lacking a voice in our society.

Therefore, in my administration, I intend to outlaw the possession of firearms by any of our citizens, except for police officers — and even then, only under special circumstances. Children have killed other children, police officers have killed innocent people, and the desperate have killed themselves. It has been too long that we have lived in fear of one another. Can't we all just get along? [Pause for cheering] As Albert Einstein once said, "Peace cannot

be kept by force; it can only be achieved
by understanding." And as Jimi Hendrix once
said, "When the power of love overcomes the
love of power, the world will know peace."

Castro's proposals, if implemented, were certainly enormous changes in policy: eliminating the Department of Defense altogether, banning civilian ownership of firearms, and perhaps most radical of all, limiting personal wealth.

Two Inaugurations: Two Vastly Different Horizons

On Saturday, January 20, 2029, there were two presidential inaugurals and two swearing-in ceremonies, with appropriate levels of both pomp and circumstance. In the eyes of the world and their respective countries, it was yet another step toward cementing and solemnizing the Great Separation of the United States.

The ceremony in Dallas was at 9 a.m. local time, and the one in San Francisco was at 1 p.m. local time. The ceremonies were staggered, so that networks and streaming services could broadcast both live, without conflicts.[5] To a historian such as myself, the entire day was an amazing pageant of duality, played out live on national (and even international) television.

Dallas, Texas

The Dallas inauguration was held in AT&T Stadium, home of the National Football League's Dallas Cowboys. Event managers had

---

5   The question of which ceremony should happen first was settled via a venerated American tradition: a coin toss. This event happened on December 6, 2028, shortly after the president-elects' first joint press conference, in order to allow for adequate planning time. The toss was witnessed by the two cognizant members of the former Supreme Court of the United States. The coin was a Kennedy half-dollar minted in 1964. President-elect Castro won the toss, and graciously agreed to go second.

to expand the venue's seating to its maximum capacity of 100,000 in order to accommodate the crowd. The event began with a performance by the Dallas Cowboys cheerleaders. A children's choir made up of elementary-school children from across Texas sang several selections; the enormous group of children was spread across the entire football field, holding LED candles and wearing colored shirts in a formation that for the television cameras formed the letters "ACNA" surrounded by laurel leaves. Then, Kelly Clarkson, Hilary Duff, LeAnn Rimes, Lee Ann Womack, Taylor Swift and the Lord Is Our Shepherd Singers (a 100-person choir from Pastor Robinson's megachurch) sang a medley of patriotic songs and hymns. The highlight of the event, right before President Faith spoke, was a holographic trio of dead celebrities singing "America the Beautiful": Elvis, Charlton Heston and Ronald Reagan. President Faith spoke for nearly 30 minutes. In her inaugural address, known as the famous "Three Gs speech," she gave a feel for what her new country could expect from her:

President Christine Faith's Inaugural Speech: January 20, 2029
Excerpts (from provided text):

I stand before you today at this historic event, proud to represent you working and God-fearing Americans. The silent majority; the Christian Americans. The people whose voices had been lost in Washington, D.C., ever since President Reagan left the White House. I stand before you today to make a commitment to bring back and to celebrate our Christian faith without being ashamed that we are the followers of Our Lord Jesus Christ. My people: We have won the war on Christianity — Christianity has won! [Pause for cheering.]

I stand here before you today because you elected me to create and to serve what will once again be a country that's number one in the world. We are here to go ahead and take what is needed in *order to bring back happiness to our families. I am here to make sure you can be allowed to protect your family, your home, your children, and your assets with pride, and without fear.*

Now, I want to tell you the principles which will guide me and our country. These guidelines will be reflected in our legislative priorities in the months and years to come. In a way, it's like a great-grandson of the United States Bill of Rights, which was created by our Founding Fathers. I am proud to be a Founding Mother of this new, great country, and to provide and protect some rights of our own.

Our new country is based upon the three Gs: God, Guns, and Greed.

Now, before the audience and the members of the press misinterpret my comments, allow me to clarify what I mean by each of these terms.

In the old United States of America, one of the operating principles of government was the separation between Church and State. That government was supposed to be independent from religion. And that was something the Founding Fathers made sure was part of the U.S. Constitution. Indeed, they considered it part of their great accomplishments when that principle was incorporated in the U.S. Constitution in 1786.

But the world of the Founding Fathers of the United States of America was different from ours. They lived in an era when there were no abortion clinics, no gay parades, no mosques in every community. They lived in the age of innocence when school libraries did not have paperback copies of Richard Dawkins' books available to elementary school students. In what country, I ask you, should children — children! — be allowed to read a book called The God Delusion? [Pause for cheering.]

The Founding Fathers lived in an age when there was no Hollywood. When there was no internet, no instant messaging, no Facebook. They truly lived in the Age of Innocence.

The Founding Fathers were right about many things, but part of their great experiment in separating Church and State was misguided.

Mr. Madison lived in an era when there were not abortion clinics on every block where thousands of fetuses would be terminated.

Mr. Jefferson lived in an era when there were not atheist scientists speaking highly of Charles Darwin and denying the hand of God in creation.

The Founding Fathers wanted to separate government from religion. Unfortunately, this is something we can't afford to do anymore. Therefore, we are a new nation, and we are proud to be a Christian Nation. We are proud to call ourselves Christians. It is this centrality of Christian values that allows me today to announce two major changes.

First: I am pleased to tell you we will eliminate the Department of Education — which meshes nicely with my commitment to reduce waste and redundancy. Why should the government have a say in what your children learn? Children should be educated first at home, and parents have the right to educate their children as they please. Parents will have the freedom to instill their own values in their children, and help create and contribute to this Christian nation.

The second major change is that my administration will have a Department of Religious Affairs, in order to ensure that our government remains a Christian Nation. The secretary of the

Department of Religious Affairs will be a senior member of my Cabinet and will guide me and our nation in everything we do. The department will prepare the country to redeem the Earth from the Great Powers of Satan. This department will ensure that the church will remain active not only for the immediate corporal wellbeing of our citizens, but that also it will ensure the eternal wellbeing of our citizens.

Now, I want to talk about the second G: that is guns.

Our newly founded country is based upon the concept of freedom. Freedom from government interference, and freedom from slander and slant from liberally biased newspapers and reporters. But freedom cannot be achieved unless people have the means to protect and enforce it. Enforce it when it is necessary and without having to wait for the police. Therefore, in our new country people are given the freedom to carry handguns and rifles, and automatic weapons when necessary. They can defend themselves and their family. But of course this does not suggest that you can shoot anybody at all that you dislike. Only those you feel are a threat. It simply means, you have the discretion to exercise judgment to defend yourself.

The third G stands for Greed. It is my belief that Greed is pivotal to personal prosperity and the long-term welfare of our country. Now, I know that greed has a negative connotation [laughter], and that's why I want to take a few minutes to fully explain what I mean by the term.

Greed is the essence of what the great philosopher Ayn Rand called, "Rational Self-Interest." It is through the pursuit of self-interest that society can benefit and prosper. Greed's enemy is communism. Greed is good for the human soul, for it allows individuals to pursue that which is inherent in the human DNA:

to survive at any cost. Once a society allows its citizens to pursue greed, individuals will be inspired to thrive and prosper. Yes, it is the pursuit of greed that allows our citizens truly to shine. In our country, we will adopt laws and legislation to maximize the human ability to pursue their individual greed. And we will eliminate government's role in the area of social security, welfare and Medicare. Yes, for a few years, it will be tough. But those who will survive the transition will not need any government help because they have proved that they are fit to survive.

In that vein, of thriving and survival, I want to announce that our country will have a Department of War and its secretary will be a member of my Cabinet. Yes, a Department of War and not Defense. As we all know, the best defense is a good offense. In the old United States of America, we were afraid to tell the world that they couldn't mess with us. And many countries took advantage of our humility — or to put it another way, our "wishy-washiness." But not anymore. We are ready to claim our position in the world of civilized nations. And we will never forget that we have a God-given responsibility to create and maintain justice throughout the world; to correct all wrongs and spread the teaching of our Lord.

And now I want to end this inaugural speech with a poem by my favorite poet, Beauregard "Bubba" Geisel, the born-again Christian cousin of Dr. Seuss:

> *we sing to God a sweet melody*
>
> *that will ring out from sea to sea*
>
> *once subject to heathen law*
>
> *on our streets sinfulness we saw*

now no longer are we to be trampled down

for now the Bible's truth will be known in every town

and every school shall preach the truth

for our young impressionable youth

may our economy be blessed

in the free market's ways

starting now till the end of days

no taxes no not a single cent

this is how it shall be; we will not repent

we shall stand our ground

and stand it proud

with our guns shall protect our lives and our goods

not to mention our schools and neighborhoods

we shall stand tall awaiting Christ's return

when those who don't stand with us shall burn

so we pledge allegiance to our religion

and the righteous life we all envision

After President Faith finished her speech, Pastor Elijah Robinson gave the benediction. As the new President Faith signed the official documents of inauguration, an impressive fireworks and mortar fire display exploded high overhead, though it was daytime and hard to see. Players from the former United States Marine Corps band began to play, and the inaugural parade wound its way around downtown Dallas before returning to the capitol.[6] The inaugural ball was held at the Dallas Convention Center, in order to have enough room for everyone who wanted to attend.

San Francisco, California

President Henry Castro's inauguration was held in San Francisco's recently renovated Moscone convention center and performance venue. The event was also simulcast on the Jumbotrons at AT&T/ Sprint Park. Altogether, 110,000 people were estimated to be present.

The ceremony began with the San Francisco Girls Chorus, who sang as the dignitaries entered. Then there was a series of performances based on the history and collective culture of San Francisco. First there was dancing and drumming by a group of local Ohlone people. A mariachi band played. Then there was a performance by Chinese acrobats and ribbon dancers. A taiko group performed an athletic drumming set. Just before President Castro spoke, Tony Bennett, Bette Midler, Beyonce, Shakira, Chaz Bono, Barbra Streisand, Wyclef Jean, Stevie Wonder, Enrique Iglesias, RuPaul Charles, and Lea Salonga (either live, or shown from digital or 3D hologram recordings) sang a medley that ended with "I Left My Heart In San Francisco." President Castro spoke for nearly two hours, translating his own speech into Spanish and back as he went. He began his address by acknowledging the fact that his inauguration was so close to Martin Luther King

---

6   Thankfully, parade planners were smart enough that the route avoided the Dallas County Administration Building, which is less than a mile from the ACNA capital — and which happens to be a (renamed) notorious landmark from a rather different presidential parade.

Jr's 100th birthday.[7] Below is an excerpt from his inaugural speech, known today as the "three Ss" speech:

President Henry Castro's Inaugural Speech: January 20, 2029 Excerpts (from provided text):

As you will expect, our new nation will be quite different from that which used to be called the United States of America.

Indeed, that is the essence of our existence and why we created a new country. But while we are different, we were born from the old United States, and spring from the same principles. The Founding Fathers of the United States wrote in the Declaration of Independence that their citizens would be entitled to the "Unalienable rights" of "life, liberty, and the pursuit of happiness." We new founders of the American Republic of Compassion also firmly believe that our citizens have the right to pursue their aspirations and their dreams. To allow this to happen, this new and growing country must adhere to a few tenets.

My administration believes in the separation of Church and State. The Founding Fathers of the United States wisely chose to include this principle in the U.S. Constitution. There were factions, in the old United States, who did not agree with this principle and who tried to reverse it. But this separation of government from religion is even more relevant today, because we are a more diverse nation than we were 250 years ago. Our nation must move away from the bigotry that all too often couches itself in religious belief. There is no way that one person or organization can have a monopoly on truth; the government should not be subject to man's interpretations of any kind of scripture in matters of law. morality, or social justice. Thus it is with firm conviction that today I say I

---

7   Martin Luther King Jr. was born on January 15, 1929. However, his birthday is observed on the third Monday in January, one day before President Castro's inauguration.

will do my utmost to separate our government from the destructive forces of religious fanaticism.

But this new country will not be defined by what we are fighting against, but what we are fighting for. Our new country's existence is based upon three fundamental principles. This set of principles defines who we are as a people and a nation, and it is what will drive us in the coming years. I call them the three Ss.

Our first principle is Science.

Science will guide our country in its day-to-day operations; it will guide us in our long-range planning and in choosing our destiny. We will use science in healing our relationship with our environment; we will use science to live better and healthier lives; we will use science to help us prepare for the future. Science will help us understand our place in the universe, plan our destiny, and manage our treatment of our planet.

I am a social scientist and not an earth scientist; but I do know that while science alone may not save us, it is unlikely that we will be saved without it.

Our second guiding principle is Serenity.

As we all know, for the past 40 years, citizens of the United States were under constant fear of shootings and assaults: shootings at the workplace, at schools, in parks and in neighborhoods. These shootings undermined one of the main purposes of a modern society, which is to provide security for its citizens. While there were many different individual reasons for these shootings, they all had one thing in common: the shooting itself. The assailant had access to firearms. It was the widespread availability of handguns and assault rifles that resulted in the deaths of 55,000 Americans last year. Almost the same death toll as the number of Americans who died in the Vietnam War — during a fifteen-year period.

It is therefore my intention to ban the sale of all types of handguns, rifles and any other types of firearms. We rely on our government to provide us with national and personal safety. And if our government fails to do this, we must then, through the democratic process, change our government. We simply cannot allow individuals to decide for themselves who to shoot, whether it be premeditated or in anger, over grievances justified or unjustified. We made the decision to replace the law of the jungle with the laws of a civilized world. Humans are animals, but we also have the powers of self-awareness. We have the capacity to control our impulses, to think twice before we act, to exact civilized justice instead of brutal revenge.

Merely banning weapons is not enough to foster serenity; removing the implement of violence does not alone affect the cause. I've been a practitioner of yoga for many years, and it's brought me a wonderful sense of balance in my life. Yoga is an ancient practice that's been co-opted by people who live in gentrified neighborhoods, when in reality it should be available to all, as a simple, healthful way to help people connect their bodies and minds, develop healthy self-control, and think first of peace. Yoga, mediation, and mindfulness — folded into our education system and into the workforce — lead to self-actualization. With self-actualization, people will come to see that compassion is the highest state of mind that a human being can achieve. With increased compassion, there will be a lessening of violence and hatred.

Compassion cannot be dictated; it has to be engraved in our souls and in our thought process. Scientists have demonstrated that compassion increases as people's insecurity diminishes. To reduce insecurity, we need to address the root of insecurity. In complex industrial societies, material insecurity is a major contributing factor to an individual's mental anguish. That is why in the American Republic of Compassion, we believe in a third S as one of our guiding principles.

The third S is for Socialism.

Socialism guarantees that citizens' basic material needs will be met. Those needs are the same for everyone. In our country, we will guarantee that employment, free physical and mental health care, and free basic housing will be available — to everyone. And when people become unable to work, we will guarantee them a stable income. [Extended pause for cheering]

As you know, I spent over ten years as a college professor. An overwhelming number of my students through the years had the same aspirations and expectations from their government: all of them wanted the security of a stable and fulfilling job. A job, for them, was the key to a happy and predictable life. Well, we cannot guarantee everyone a job that will be professionally fulfilling, since people's interests are diverse and can change over the years; but we can and should provide and guarantee a stable job for every person in our country. Once we guarantee our citizens a job, we are also guaranteeing them an income and self-esteem, two things required for a healthy existence in mind and body.

Another common expectation my students had, as well as the greater population, according to polls, is national health insurance. National, single-payer health insurance. With continuous innovations in healthcare delivery and medical technology, the cost of health care keeps soaring. One major illness can financially destroy a family. The old United States was the only developed country in the world not to have a national healthcare system. It is time that we, the evolved states of the American Republic of Compassion, join the rest of the civilized world, and keep our people healthy. [Pause for cheering.]

After the cheering for the "three Ss" died down, he began diving into the third S, putting forth his most daring socialist policies of all by focusing on the active redistribution of wealth:

Now, some cynical members of our country will be questioning the practicality of my agenda. They would ask how we could afford these ambitious goals. My answer is simple. The problem with the financial system of the old United States was not a lack of financial resources; the issue was misdistribution. Wealth was concentrated in the hands of a few: some were hard-working people, and some were just fortunate people; still others were people with fortunate families, who were neither hard-working nor terribly deserving of their fortunes. And it was this misdistribution that created our systemic poverty.

How systemic was this poverty? Beginning with the turn of the century and by the mid-2020s, the income of the top 1% of Americans grew by 800%. Yet, the income of America's middle class grew by a mere 15%. Eight hundred percent compared with just fifteen percent.

And the poorest people in our country? During the same period, the income of the poorest 20% grew by only 8%. eight percent. More than 90% of the growth in U.S. wealth since 1983 went to the top 10% of Americans. This is what I mean by misdistribution of wealth.

Between 2000 and 2010, the income of an average American family of four (parents and two children) remained almost constant at about $55,000. Say this family was interested in computers, in *educating their children. That's a noble goal, right? Well, in 2000, this family bought a word processing program for about $75. At that time, the CEO of the company selling these products had a net worth of $52 billion. Say that CEO wasn't satisfied with his $52 billion (and yes, "his" — we can be pretty sure that in 2000 the CEO of a computer company was a straight white man). [Pause for laughter.]*

Ten years later, the family was still making $55,000; but now the CEO's changed his product. Now it's a subscription — and it costs $195 per year. In the meantime, the wealth of the same CEO soared from $52 billion to $65 billion. This is what I mean by misdistribution of wealth. Does it really make a difference to that CEO who's worth $52 billion to keep thinking of ways to siphon off money from a family that has an annual income of $55,000? Does this CEO really ... need ... the additional $10 billion? [Pause for laughter, boos, jeering.]

Often the answer is not financial; rather, the accumulation of wealth itself was recognized as success in our country. Our old country.

President Castro went on to propose another major social innovation: making community service not just a fundamental value, but a national obligation:

We need to create a new definition of success. Success in the ARC will not be based upon how much wealth we accumulate. Success will not be based upon the size of our yachts, the number of our airplanes, or the size of our houses. Success will be based on the lives we touch. It will be based, not upon how much we take, but how much we give.

That is why today, I am announcing that we will create a Department of Volunteerism and Community Service. The secretary of this department will be an important member of my Cabinet.

Yes, the measure of success in the American Republic of Compassion will be the amount that we all give back to our communities. And that is why each individual will be required to do one full day of volunteer work a week in his/her community. That applies to everyone, regardless of their job and their position. Yes, even the CEO of that computer company. [Laughter]

How will we afford to implement this dramatic social agenda? Simple: we will not have a military force. This may come as a shock to you, but the former United States of America spent nearly half its federal budget on the Department of Defense. Well, we won't need a Department of Defense, because we are not planning to invade any country; nor are we expecting to be invaded by any country. We will invest that money on improving our educational system, on providing health care and jobs for our citizens. And that will be the essence of our strength. Yes. The happiness of our citizens is the best defense we can have against any potential enemy, and an educated population is the best equipment a nation can possess.

When Castro finished his speech and signed the official inaugural document, there was a trumpet fanfare and paper streamers exploded from confetti cannons as the crowd in attendance went crazy. The members of Sister Sledge came onstage, along with Aretha Franklin and Beyoncé, backed up by the San Francisco Gay Men's Chorus, and sang "We are Family," while the crowd sang along. President Castro and Vice President Wong each sang a verse on mic, to shrieks of surprise and delight from the crowd, and then all the singers from the ceremony streamed onstage and there was a dance party. Wong and Castro led the inaugural parade down Market Street to United Nations Plaza where there was an afterparty for the public; the official Inaugural Ball was held near City Hall at the Bill Graham Civic Auditorium.

Ideologically, the two inaugurations and respective inaugural speeches solidified the two countries' new directions: Faith's "three Gs" — God, guns, and greed — stood in stark contrast to Castro's "three Ss" — science, serenity, and socialism. Each administration could at last make the major, life-altering policy decisions that they'd been promising and threatening to make for years, under the Pre-Separation United States. Now, finally unfettered by political opposition, each country was free to pursue its own goals, full speed ahead.

Officially, the two inaugurations granted each new country, the ARC and the ACNA, the pomp and circumstance and the outward trappings of statehood. As for the day-to-day logistical business of statehood, including numerous questions involving active court cases, interstate and now international commerce, the two countries and their respective peoples were essentially "muddling through," making decisions as they arose, or postponing them if necessary. After all, the first president of the United States was inaugurated in the year 1789, but the Bill of Rights, that set of ten amendments upon which so much of our founding mythology was based, was not even successfully ratified until 1791. The federal government had already been operational for two years before the first ten amendments were officially made law of the land — and many of the states had governments and constitutions already, which predated the U.S. Constitution and federal government.

Post-Separation, the people, the states, and the new federal governments, were doing what they had always been doing: figuring it out as they went along.

PART TWO

Sibling Rivalry:
Developing the ACNA and the ARC

CHAPTER FIVE

First Steps to New Government

"We are America and those other people are not."

- Rich Bond, 1992
Chairman of the Republican National Committee

"Democrats are the 'enemy of normal Americans.'"

- Newt Gingrich, Speaker of the House, 1995-1999

*"Suppose you were an idiot. And suppose you were a Republican.
But I repeat myself."*

- Harry S. Truman, 1948 (campaign speech)

"[W]e'll be running in this election this year against a party almost exactly opposite from us - a party with a narrow vision, a party afraid of the future"

- Jimmy Carter, 1980 (remarks at a DNC fundraising dinner)

THE ACNA AND ITS FRATERNAL twin the ARC were similarly growing up, and, like real children, were showing their differences as they grew. Also like many real siblings, they remained skeptical and suspicious of each other. Blues, as a rule, tend to be more skeptical than Reds, especially when it comes to their own ideals, so they were wary of both their own success and of ACNA's. Contrariwise, Reds are more skeptical of Blues than Blues are of Reds, so the ridicule toward ARC from over the border was loud and clear.

Would the non-religious ARC have enough moral and social cohesion to function effectively as a country, Red critics jeered? Would the state-sponsored Christians of ACNA all shoot each other in the first month, Blue critics wondered? Could either government deliver on their promises, so carefully outlined in their inaugural speeches, or were those promises simply empty statements? Would real change indeed come? Cynics and zealots alike watched closely as the two fledgeling governments stretched their wings and began to crow.

Building A New Government: ACNA

Having been sworn in officially as president of the ACNA, Christine Faith immediately set to work putting together her official government, modifying the Pre-Separation U.S. federal structure where necessary to make it her own.

The Legislative Branch of the government was mostly taken care of; legislators from the ACNA states were moving into their offices, transferring staffers and papers and furniture from their Washington, D.C., location to Dallas.

The Judicial Branch was also in process: Justice James Propert (backed up by his personal assistant) was serving as Official Temporary Chief Justice, again with the understanding that he would help appoint the ACNA Supreme Court and then retire. According to reports, however, he found it difficult to search out judicial candidates who met his specific criteria, and even more difficult to deal with the idea of eventual retirement. Candidate after candidate was rejected, and often left his office wiping away tears. Therefore, in the interim Chief Justice Propert had decided to hear cases by himself, assisted by clerks.

President Faith's Cabinet mostly resembled a Pre-Separation Cabinet, except for a few differences and one major substitution. As promised in her inaugural address, there was no Department of Education, because the functions that previously were fulfilled by the Pre-Separation Department of Education were now the responsibility of the Department of Religious Activities. She also rearranged the order of succession within the Cabinet, moving toward the top of the hierarchy those departments that were more important to her government platform. Hence, President Faith's Cabinet was as follows, in order of succession to the presidency:

- Vice president
- Secretary of State
- Secretary of Homeland Security
- Secretary of the Treasury
- Secretary of War
- Secretary of Energy
- Secretary of Religious Affairs
- Attorney General
- Secretary of Commerce
- Secretary of the Interior
- Secretary of Agriculture

- Secretary of Labor
- Secretary of Health and Human Services
- Secretary of Housing and Urban Development
- Secretary of Transportation
- Secretary of Veterans Affairs.

Her most significant Cabinet position was the new one: the Secretary of Religious Affairs. Earlier rumors about a political deal between Christine Faith and Pastor Elijah Robinson proved to be true when President Faith announced that she was appointing the pastor as the new secretary of Religious Affairs. From the initial announcement of this decision it was clear that the Department of Religious Affairs was going to be very influential in Faith's Administration. Pastor/Secretary Robinson wasted no time at all in making his influence clear, as in his remarks in a speech at Liberty University. The speech was live-tweeted by most of the audience and several administration staffers, released on YouTube moments after its completion, and the Department of Religious Affairs released a transcript on its website and as a press release a few days later.

Excerpt from the press release:
ACNA Department of Religious Affairs
FOR IMMEDIATE RELEASE — February 4, 2029
> *Secretary Pastor Elijah Robinson Gives Speech to Liberty University students*

> *DATELINE: Lynchburg, VA   Pastor/Secretary Robinson stated: "One of the things that defines our new country is that it is a Christian nation. And we won't be ashamed to admit it. The teachings of Our Lord will guide us in our daily life and will help us to decide who is our friend and who is our enemy. Since we are now, praise the Lord, a Christian nation, we are also a nation of Christian states, and those states should be made up of good, moral, righteous Christian people.*

Therefore, I have asked all our states to require mandatory Bible and religious education during the first hour of the day in every school in every grade, from kindergarten all the way through high school. Compliance with this mandate would make states eligible for financial grants from the Department of Religious Affairs. We will also need to work on rolling back the clock on some adjudication of certain marriage rights that we believe contradict Christian teachings, but that is not our first priority."

The headline was merely the fact that Robinson, the new secretary, gave a speech, but of course the real news was the announcement of the new mandatory religious education policy. Most of the attendees of the speech and others who tweeted quotes and comments were ecstatic about the news. The more clear-headed wondered aloud about the details: would there be textbooks issued, or would the Bible alone be enough? And what version of the Bible? Would teachers' particular sects of Christianity influence their teaching of the Bible in schools, or would they receive standardized training? Would parents have a say in what their child learned in religion class? Pastor Robinson replied with the vague but reassuring statement, "The Lord Shall Provide."

Building a New Government: ARC

After having been sworn in officially as president of the ARC, Henry Castro immediately set to work putting together his own official federal government. As did ACNA, the ARC government left the legislative branch of the government largely untouched. The Blue state senators and representatives were all busy moving their offices and temporary residences across the country; since real estate was hard to come by in San Francisco, legislators' offices and residences were installed in the Presidio, in the unused military barracks with a gorgeous view of San Francisco Bay.

As for the Executive Branch, Castro made similar changes to the structure of his Cabinet. From his inaugural speech and other public statements, it seemed that President Henry Castro had a genuine interest in improving his people's quality of life. But the media wondered: how does the government indeed know whether any given organization or policy is indeed treating people with compassion? Several universities in the ARC held symposia to study and investigate the idea, with topics such as "What Is Compassion?" "Loving Me, Loving You," and "Compassion: One Singular Sensation." One school of thought, attributed to an industrial psychologist working for the Disney Corporation, argued that compassionate public policy over a long period of time would increase people's level of happiness. Thus, it did not come as surprise to the attentive public when on May 15, 2029, the government of President Castro announced the creation of a new federal agency, with a Cabinet-level secretary, which was responsible for implementing governmental policy related to public happiness. The new agency, the Bureau of Public Happiness, would serve as an advocate for citizens' happiness and would provide official guidelines to ensure that people's levels of happiness measured up to those suggested by the government. The agency was also given the responsibility of developing an index for measuring happiness and ensuring that individual as well as societal levels of happiness met the minimum level set by government.

With the creation of the Bureau of Personal Happiness, President Castro finished putting together his Cabinet, which was, like President Faith's, also shaped mostly like the traditional Pre-Separation Cabinet. Again, parallel to President Faith, President Castro also did some rearranging and a little renaming as well, moving those Cabinet positions that were closer to his heart closer to the top of the hierarchy. His Cabinet, in order of succession to the presidency:

- Vice president
- Secretary of State
- Secretary of Education

- Secretary of Health and Wellbeing
- Secretary of Personal Happiness
- Secretary of Labor
- Secretary of the Treasury
- Secretary of Energy
- Attorney General
- Secretary of Commerce
- Secretary of the Interior
- Secretary of Agriculture
- Secretary of Labor
- Secretary of Housing and Urban Development
- Secretary of Volunteerism and Community Service
- Secretary of Transportation
- Secretary of Veterans Affairs

Constructing a Judicial Branch was in process: Justice Catherine Kaginmore was serving as Official Temporary Chief Justice, tasked with helping to appoint nine members of a new Supreme Court. Justice Kaginmore immediately set about fulfilling her dream court, of nine women Supreme Court justices. She had never forgotten the famous remarks by Justice Ruth Bader Ginsburg at the 10th Circuit Bench & Bar Conference in 2012: "[W]hen I'm sometimes asked, when will there be enough [women on the Supreme Court]? And I say when there are nine, people are shocked. But there'd been nine men, and nobody's ever raised a question about that."

She would also not be moved in the sense of retiring; though originally both she and Justice James Propert had agreed to appoint new supreme courts in the two countries and then retire, neither of them wanted to give up the chance to shape a country's judicial system. The ARC commissioned an official portrait of her, as the First Chief Justice of ARC and the First Female Chief Justice in the history of the States on the American Continent, and upon viewing images of the finished portrait, one could not help but notice the spark of satisfaction in her eyes.

Media: The Game of Groans

As two new brands trying to establish themselves on the world stage, each new country had a publicity problem. In order to seem like they had an equal amount of legitimacy, the two countries were jockeying for position, each trying to match the other country's visibility and prestige. As each new country developed, they wanted to make sure that their national message was clear and different from the old one — and slightly stronger than their sister country's. As a result, they ended up matching each other in terms of actions and even in terms of venue. Each new president was making the rounds of network and cable TV, and wanted to be interviewed by the same interviewers. Take, for example, these two interviews, both conducted by veteran political commentator Gill O'Really of Fox News.

O'Really announced that he would interview President Castro on a live broadcast at 8 p.m. on February 2, 2029. Below is an excerpt from a transcript of Mr. O'Really's interview with President Castro:

O'REALLY: Mr. President — are you a president, is that the right title? Sure, I guess you are — before we start this interview, I would like to provide you with an opportunity to respond to the charges in the media that the American Republic of Compassion is a front for the People's Republic of China. Now, I'm not saying I believe it, but these charges have been leveled by those who have made a connection between similarity of the abbreviation for your country's name, which is ARC, and the abbreviation for the People's Republic of China, which is PRC. Also, an investigation by the Donald Trump Foundation for Citizenship Verification has made accusations that you are the illegitimate son of former Cuban dictator Fidel Castro and that your vice president's parents were actually born in the People's Republic of China and not in the U.S., and that she still has cousins and other relatives there. How would you respond to these charges?

CASTRO: First of all, Gill, the intimation that our country took its name as an inspiration from the People's Republic of China is ridiculous; it would be like asking whether the ACNA took as inspiration the word "acne," say. Merely because it is similar, it doesn't mean it's the same. Actually, the name of our country was chosen by the people, during our campaign. Last fall, we asked the nation to send us their views of what our campaign platform stood for. "Compassion" was a word that came up over and over. We saw it in millions of Facebook posts, tweets, emails, Instagrams, Snapchats, bogles ... over every social media platform. But the actual name of the country was cemented in the public eye when the host of the Daily Show referred to me as the president of the American Republic of Compassion. We thought it was a wonderful and accurate depiction of our political ideology. And our people seemed to like it. So we took that as the name of our new country.

Now, in regard to the second part of your question, I simply say: it's nonsense. We are not a front for another country. We are a front for humanity and social justice. Vice President Wong and I are Americans. We were born in America, on American soil. Vice President Wong's parents were born in Taiwan which at some point in the distant past was part of China — though Taiwan still refuses to acknowledge that. So, of course it's quite natural for her to have relatives in China. I hear you have relatives in Germany and Ireland, Gill ... does that make you a European? [Chuckles.] In regard to my background, I have no connection to Fidel Castro. In fact, for your information, I have never even smoked a cigar in my life. But I have nothing to hide — so maybe the Foundation should look into my relatives as well ... [laughs].

The interviewer had a slightly different tone during his interview with the ACNA secretary of Religious Affairs, which one may observe from reading an excerpt from the transcript:

Text of Secretary Elijah Robinson's interview with Mr. Gill O'Really, from Fox Network, on February 10, 2029.

O'REALLY: Well, Pastor Robinson, thank you for joining us today. Before we begin this interview, I would like to provide you with an opportunity to comment on various rumors in the media that suggest you are related to the infamous Mrs. Robinson who was portrayed in a movie in the late 1960s. Our viewers want to know: is this true?

ROBINSON: Thanks, Gill, and please, call me Mr. Secretary. [Laughter] Gill, I appreciate this opportunity to clear this issue. Now, hold on to your hat: you might be surprised to learn that yes, I am indeed the son of a Mrs. Robinson. And yes, she was that Mrs. Robinson. And she was indeed so badly portrayed by Hollywood in that movie. I think she was a misunderstood individual. [inaudible] I am proud to be her son and I attribute all of my moral and religious beliefs to what I learned from her when I was growing up in California. She was a lovely Christian woman, and that godless heathen liberal young man took advantage of her. People may not know that my mother went to church every Sunday and raised money for the Salvation Army during the holidays. She was indeed a Christian who felt the presence of God throughout her life.

O'REALLY: Thank you, Pastor — I mean, Mr. Secretary. [Laughter] Now, I'd like to ask you a few questions about your vision for the education of our young people in our new country. More specifically, I would like to ask you about the new programs you're working on. Religious education in schools? Everyone's talking about it! Many people are saying, finally, finally! What do you have up your sleeve, there?

ROBINSON: Sure, Gill. In the upcoming months we will establish a prayer-in-school program from kindergarten through high school. We will also establish mandatory religious education for every grade level. No longer will we allow our youths to be corrupted by amoral secular learning which confuses our children and threatens our faith. Whereas some see the incorporation of religious education into our academic curriculum as somehow some kind of [air quotes] "threat," I see it as the separation of the wheat from the chaff, or the separation of the lambs from the goats. Too long we have sat idly by as our faith was assaulted by those who do not accept the truth. It is time we took a stand for truth, a stand for Jesus.

O'REALLY: So, is there a particular denomination of Christianity that will be incorporated in the mandatory religious classes?

ROBINSON: Well, Gill, you know we're a Protestant nation, right? [chuckle] And as a Protestant nation, we refuse to submit to the authority of Rome, or should I say lack thereof. As a man who has dedicated his life to Christ and the Bible, I find it abundantly clear that religion is between an individual and God, and there's no need for the church to mediate.

O'REALLY: That sounds contradictory, coming from the man who is now in charge of an entire nation's religious wellbeing. There are thousands of Protestant denominations. Can you please specify which one the educational system will adhere to?

ROBINSON: In this religious education program I'm speaking of, Gill, we will adhere to the idea that faith alone is the determinant of salvation. You have to be faithful from the inside out. If you have faith in Christ, you can be saved. You can't learn it by doing [air quotes] "good works," and you can't "pretend" to be saved by following rules, like, you know, wearing certain clothes or eating certain foods, or *not* wearing certain clothes and *not* eating certain foods. We will teach our children the truth: That humanity is totally depraved, due to original sin. That the Bible is a literal revelation from God to humanity. That had it not been for the sacrifice of Jesus no man can taste salvation. Other than that, we will not place a label on our religion; everyone is free to practice the Christian faith of their choosing. Classes will stick to individual topics and their relation to the teachings in the Bible.

O'REALLY: Do you plan on openly teaching that evolution has not occurred and that the universe was created in six days?

ROBINSON: Come on now, Gill, that's a silly question. I thought you knew me better than that. Since my coming to Christ and my acceptance of the complete and utter truth of the Bible, I have found that there is no room for evolution in the Genesis account of creation. I will throw the whole weight of my authority in removing evolution from schools, but more importantly I will remove it from the minds of our youths.

O'REALLY: There is staunch opposition from the Watchtower Society regarding your teachings on the Trinity. Can you please respond to this?

ROBINSON: Now, Gill. The Jehovah's Witnesses are entitled to their beliefs. At the same time, most Christians don't adhere to their specific beliefs, and nor should we. They don't believe in the

Trinity, and therefore they don't believe that Jesus was God or part of God, and I just don't hold with that. I am not a prophet. I am merely a pillar of authority dedicating myself to upholding the morality of our great nation.

O'REALLY: What about those young people who question the mandatory religious education? Or who still want to learn about evolution? What's your policy there?

ROBINSON: Evolution is a theory that won't die soon. It has been corrupting our society for many years now. As for the youths who are drawn to it, we'll just have to pray for 'em and teach 'em what the Bible says about creation, 'cause that's the truth.

Astute readers will notice that O'Really failed to press Pastor Secretary Robinson on the issue of multiple Christian sects. The Watchtower Society is one of many, many Christian denominations and ecclesiastical traditions in existence — by some counting methods, there are upward of 33,000 worldwide. Though they may all profess to be "Christian," differences in rite, doctrine and beliefs (no matter how minute) are possible at every level, and human beings with similar but distinct interests can always find points on which to disagree. As web cartoonist Randall Munroe once pointed out, "Human subcultures are nested fractally. There's no bottom." Though Pastor Secretary Robinson sidestepped O'Really's question, this historian can only imagine that once ACNA's religious education programs are fully implemented and functioning nationwide, the inter-Christian bickering can fully begin. With all the guns currently in the hands of ACNA citizens, this historian hopes that resolving the religious differences in ACNA will take a more friendly path than those among Protestants and Catholics in 20th Century Northern Ireland, or centuries of bloody feuds between Islamic sects Sunnis and Shiites, which are still ongoing.

Solving Problems: War and Peace

Given ACNA's commitment to a very strong military and yet the government's commitment to a very low tax rate (10% across the board), President Faith made a bold and creative move to reconcile the two positions. Early in her administration, in February 2029, she approved a request made by her newly appointed Secretary of War Steve Janney: outsourcing the country's military. Secretary Janney made the formal televised announcement to the press and the public, sunlight reflecting off his bald head as he spoke from the roof of the ACNA capital building:

Television Address
ACNA Department of Homeland Security
Secretary Steve Janney (February 1, 2029)

> *The Armed Christian Nations of America is committed to a very strong military. We are committed not just to maintaining our cultural and economic interests worldwide, but also to expanding those interests. In fact, we have a moral duty to expand our interests, because we were given that responsibility by God. No doubt this responsibility requires that we keep and maintain a strong military, with state-of-the-art equipment. However, we are also committed to reducing taxes and keeping our nation and our people out of harm's way. We believe that our own promising youths should spend their time serving as soldiers of Christ, spreading the word of the Gospel. These two objectives have led us to a very logical conclusion. We must outsource the most dangerous parts of our War Department. We must reduce the risk of death to our young people. Why not leave the strategic defense of our country to professionals? Through outsourcing, we will be able to reduce the cost of defending our country and at the same time phase out expenses associated with taking care of our veterans.*

Now, some may criticize our plan, saying, "It can't be done!" Well, these people have forgotten that during the presidency of George W. Bush, we did exactly that. We hired a company called Blackwater. Through the contract with Blackwater the government was able to accomplish its objectives without having to jump through a lot of political hoops, without having to sit around and talk about should they, shouldn't they, is it right, is it wrong. They could just get down to business.

But there was one problem with that plan. Given the fact that Blackwater was a private company, it cost the country a lot of money — more than it would have if their efforts were run by the Department of Defense. Therefore, our new contract will be with India, the largest democracy in the world and our important global ally. By outsourcing certain parts of our military with the Indian company Maharaja Limited, we can get first-rate and dedicated manpower, augmented with our technology, at a fraction of the cost.

This cooperative venture will also help to strengthen India so it can stop Chinese expansion, and control other threats in the region. Another benefit of working with India, a nuclear country, is that we will even be able to collaborate in matters related to nuclear weapons, should that be needed.

For a cost of just $2,500 a year per soldier, ACNA had explored a preliminary multiyear arrangement with a company in India that could provide combat-ready troops on demand. A low-ranking officer would cost $3500-$4,000 per year on average, while higher-ranking officers would all come from ACNA's Department of War. The company would be responsible for all military equipment and related infrastructure. Granted, these prices were quoted as base prices, for maintaining soldiers during peacetime, and don't include other bells and whistles. But still, the approximate average cost per soldier per year in Afghanistan being around $815,000, it is fair to say that even considering differences of wartime and peacetime, outsourcing would still result in a staggering discount.

In finishing the address, Janney added one final comment, clips of which went viral online:

> *I will close this address by emphasizing that, per an official agreement between the ACNA and the ARC, our Department of War will protect ARC from any possible foreign attacks in the future, since apparently the ARC will be abandoning its Department of Defense.*

Watching the video clip, it is easy to discern the look and tone of disgust and ridicule from Secretary Janney, as he spoke about the ARC's plans to dismantle its Defense Department. Political spin doctors rushed to defend the clip, but the damage had been done.

Checks and Balances?

Creating a new country gave each respective government a chance to start over from scratch, making it possible to change not only the structure of the Cabinet, but the very government itself. As soon as the states officially split into two countries, political scholars on all sides speculated about the possible relationship between each country's executive and legislative branches.

Given the strong emphasis the ACNA placed on war and individual aggression, some analysts predicted that ACNA's political structure could become very similar to that of such countries as Saudi Arabia, where political power rested exclusively in the executive branch, and that there would soon no longer be an independent legislative branch in the newly created country. Perhaps President Faith sought to prove these speculations wrong, when she and the leaders of the ACNA House of Representatives and Senate issued a joint communique affirming their adherence to true representative government, where power was divided among the two branches.

ACNA Offices of the President And Senate And House of Representatives

FOR IMMEDIATE RELEASE — February 5, 2029

Joint Communiqué Affirming Commitment to Representative Government

The government of ACNA, consisting of the president and its legislative branch, has reached an agreement regarding the frequency and duration of the legislative sessions. Our agreement will cut out the wasteful elements of the previous government, leading to a more efficient legislative process. Agreeing to the principles of shared governance, yet cognizant of the demands on the time of our hard-working congressmen and senators, we have reached an agreement that that there is no need for our legislative branch to actually meet in Dallas. Since our country is committed to using the most sophisticated technologies, we have decided that our congressmen and senators can fulfill their responsibilities by conducting their work via the internet.

Now, instead of drafting legislation and then having it revised by our lobbyists, for the sake of efficiency we will have approved lobbyists, or "law writers," draft the legislation. Our legislators will then register their approval or disapproval in person or online. This should provide for an efficient governmental process, cutting out endless rounds of revision and debate. This structure will free our congressmen and senators to devote full time to fundraising, quantitatively assessing the will of their constituents, which is the primary responsibility of elected officials. And finally, through adopting this new structure we will reduce the cost of running the government, since we have no need to construct extensive office and meeting space for the entire House and the Senate.

ACNA's "efficient legislature" announcement left pundits raising their eyebrows. ARC's government responded only obliquely, by posting pictures of themselves enjoying the view of the Golden Gate Bridge from their offices and apartments, from official state barbecues at Marina Green and Chrissy Field, and from state cocktail parties held on Alcatraz. The idea was to show legislators all in the same location, having fun together. Even President Castro's official social media accounts posted a picture of himself and the First Gentleman playing Ultimate Frisbee with members of the House and Senate, with the caption: "Work together, work as a team. ARC FTW! "[1]

Meanwhile, one political commentator on MSNBC commented that "applications to be an ACNA law-writer must be pretty expensive, indeed."

Defending a New Country

One of the issues that got a great deal of media attention during the Pre-Separation presidential election in 2028 was national defense: the two parties differed from each other in how they would hypothetically protect the country from a terrorist attack such as the one that took place in the United States in 2001. Though an attack on that scale had not been repeated, the specter still loomed, and journalists and debate moderators were quick to confront candidates with the question during the protracted election process.

---

1   Acronym here is "For the Win." Online, FTW has a number of other meanings as well.

The people of ACNA were relieved when they read the secretary of Homeland Security's blog entry (shared virally on social media) for February 8, 2029. The accompanying graphic was a photoshopped image of Janney, bushy eyebrows raised, aiming an assault rifle at a matador waving a blue cape.

Official Blog, Department of Homeland Security
Posted by: Secretary Steve Janney (February 8, 2029)
"Yesterday, I met with Secretary Pastor Robinson of the Department of Religious Affairs to coordinate our security efforts. After considerable discussion, we realized that the time is gone when we needed to worry about the "Red Scare"; the threat of communism and communist countries is long past. Nowadays, we need to worry about everyone: Muslims, gays, Chinese, Japanese, North Koreans, Cubans, atheists and Hollywood producers. We like to call this the 'Blue Scare.'

"The only way we can achieve total security is for citizens to be suspicious of everyone and be prepared to act when they need to act. This can happen when everyone is armed and able to act with vigilance and courage. We already have extensive laws in place protecting every citizen's right to own and carry firearms. But we can do even more, to accomplish the objective of total security. One of the principles, or guiding values, of the ACNA is self-determination. This concept was based upon the notion that in a civilized and modern society, individuals should have the power to control their own destinies. And individuals, I'm told, are able to distinguish right from wrong starting at about the age of six or seven. Therefore, the Department of Homeland Security will work with the Department of Religious Affairs to create a K-12 curriculum in the use of self-defense, including instruction in the use of assault rifles, and honing skills in identifying suspicious individuals and situations."

Perhaps his handlers took down the blog entry, for it disappeared within a week, though it had already gone viral across global social media. On his blog, the post was replaced by a more staid announcement of the K-12 defense program — without a graphic.

A few days later, the Department of the Interior released another official announcement, which further confirmed ACNA's commitment to a life of vigilance and security.

ACNA Department of Interior
FOR IMMEDIATE RELEASE: March 1, 2029
Announcement From Secretary David Crockett

The Department of the Interior, in cooperation with the departments of Defense and Homeland Security, has authorized hospitality chains operating within our country's national park and national monuments to provide their guests with complimentary use of handguns for the duration of their visits. This measure would assure that our people can visit our parks and monuments with complete peace of mind and that they are not subject to fear and intimidation while away from their homes. Because national parks and monuments are public land, they belong to members of the public, and thus the principles of stand-your-ground apply to those places: a person has a right to be there and thus no duty to retreat in case of threat to life or limb. Additionally, the Department will extend the principle of stand-your-ground to temporary residences such as motels, hotels and campsites.

President Faith and her administration were fully committed to ensuring that the citizens of her country were truly safe, while at the same time empowering them to act when they needed to act quickly and not have to wait for the government's response. With these announcements, ACNA was paving the road to security, as they prepared to arm both tourists and children, even providing handguns for temporary personal use on vacation. Firearms were to become a part of daily life, with easy access no matter where you were in the country. Thus, they reasoned, daily life would soon become as safe as possible.

Meanwhile, in the ARC, the opposite trend was happening. Whereas the ACNA was invested in arming and empowering their citizens, the ARC was actively trying to build a safe and gentle society through emotional empowerment. Compassion is defined by Wikipedia, bastion of all knowledge, as "The response to the suffering of others that motivates a desire to help." Who, specifically, would be the "others," and how would the government, rather than private individuals, provide "help?"

The first sign of what compassion meant in the new republic appeared in a speech by Secretary of Health and Wellbeing Tara Kaiser on March 12, 2029. Speaking at the National Association of Farm Workers in Spokane, Washington, Kaiser gave a televised speech in front of 800 farm owners, farmworkers, and other agricultural executives. From the official transcript:

KAISER: Ladies and Gentlemen, I am pleased to announce today the adoption of an important public policy proposal which President Castro's Cabinet has approved, and which will be introduced to our legislative branch next week. The initiative consists of a number of proposals that will phase out the eating of animals over the next ten years.

Our initiative is based upon two considerations. First, as a country that is based upon compassion, we cannot accept the killing of animals solely for people's consumption. Further, our initiative is based upon some of the most recent medical considerations and the health and environmental benefits of a vegetarian diet

— especially when it is applied to a large swath of the Earth's population.

While there are variations in the diets of individual vegetarians, the term broadly implies the abstinence from animal flesh in one's diet. Throughout the ages, many civilizations and groups of people have been vegetarian, and the practice is common and widespread in many countries today, but vegetarians have often been a global minority.

People have chosen the vegetarian diet for a variety of reasons. Some people are vegetarians for health reasons. Others have a moral or spiritual basis for their vegetarian diet: to prevent animal suffering and death, to protest interconnected forms of oppression, to foster inter-species kinship and compassion, and to promote universal nonviolence, or "ahimsa." [Kaiser performs the "namaste" prayer gesture.] Still others have a social reason: to benefit the environment, or to protest the manipulation of nature, world hunger and social injustice.

Now, this is not a decision driven in any way by religion. As you are aware, one of the founding principles of the ARC is the separation between Church and State. But we also know that many of you, in your personal lives, belong to the Christian faith. That is something totally personal, and the government will not interfere in that relationship. But just in case it means something to you personally, according to some interpretations of Christian moral thought, vegetarianism is preferred. This connection was eloquently expressed in Dostoevsky's The Brothers Karamazov when Father Zosima points out that a strong love of God also extends to animals:

"Love God's creation, love every atom of it separately, and love it also as a whole; love every green leaf, every ray of God's light; love the animals and the plants and every inanimate object. If you come to love all things, you will perceive God's mystery inherent in all things; once you have perceived it, you will understand it better and better every day. And finally you will love the world with a total universal love.

"Love the animals: God has given them the beginnings of thought and untroubled joy. So do not disturb their joy, do not torment them, do not deprive them of their wellbeing, do not work against God's intent. Man, do not pride yourself on your superiority to the animals, for they are without sin, while you, with all your greatness, you defile the earth wherever you appear and leave an ignoble trail behind you."

As for the lingering question of ARC's national defense strategy — which was not an unreasonable one, considering the Castro government pledged to eliminate both firearms from the populace but also the Defense Department from the government — they went to the media to explain their new plan. The Office of the President released an official cartoon-style video, narrated by Vice President Wong and her teenage daughter Zora. Animated in a friendly cut-paper style, the meat of the text ran as follows (from the official screenplay):

ZORA:
Mom, will we be safe?

WONG:

Zora, are you having nightmares again? You're way too old for that.

ZORA:

No, mom … I mean, will our new country be safe?

WONG:

Of course, honey. In this country we all take care of each other, remember?

ZORA:

But what if there are, you know … people out to get us?

WONG:

Don't worry about that, honey. They may be out to get us, but we're smarter than they are.

[animation of map and little buildings flying between countries]

[WONG CONTINUES]

When our country split from the ACNA, the two new countries reached a preliminary agreement. ACNA will keep most of the assets of the old Pentagon and the Department of Defense, and the ARC will take NASA, the

National Science Foundation, the National Institutes of Health, the Department of Education, and other science-based assets.

[animation of ARC and ACNA presidents signing a treaty and shaking hands]

[WONG CONTINUES]

Each country made a promise to take care of these capabilities, expand upon them, and provide them to its sister country if needed. In other words, ARC will help ACNA if it needs the services of NASA and other science agencies, and, in return, ACNA will provide defense capabilities to ARC, if or when requested by ARC.

[friendly animation of battle]

[WONG CONTINUES]

Our government has reached an agreement with President Faith that, should there ever be an aggression from a foreign country against ARC, we can count on full support from ACNA and NATO, the North Atlantic Treaty Organization.

ZORA:

Like … another World War? Who'd be silly
enough to start one of those?

<u>WONG:</u>
Exactly, dear. Now finish your homework.

Official Trappings: Creating a Brand

Quite apart from policy changes, if these two countries were to
have international visibility and branding, it was obvious that they
each needed to have a flag and a seal — even if the duration of either
new political entity was brief. Flags represent a country's political
identity, and the solid red and solid blue flags used in the interim had
been functional but unimpressive.

The ARC, having a higher population of artists and designers,
took the first steps toward creating a flag. President Castro, as one
who professes a deep belief in involving the citizens of his country
in major governmental decisions, released an internet video asking
for input for the design of the flag. The video was released a few days
after his inauguration, and the famous "three Ss speech," timed to
capitalize on the momentum of the sentiment and the catchphrase.
In a cheeky homage to serene PBS artist Bob Ross, Castro was filmed
in front of a black background next to an easel, wearing overalls and
holding an oversize acrylic palette. On the easel was, instead of a
blank canvas, a rectangular blue flag. After muddling some paint on
the palette with a brush, Castro turned to the camera, smiled, and
spoke:

<u>CASTRO:</u>

Think about what this new country stands for.
Think about our commitment to the three Ss:
Science, Serenity and Socialism. Think about
what images you'd like to represent this
new country, this republic of compassion.
My countrypeople: submit your ideas for
our new flag to YouTube, in the comments
below, and make your voice heard. My staff
will read every single comment, so don't be
afraid to tell us your opinion. [Picking up
some paint.] Hmm, maybe it needs a happy
little tree …

Alphabet, parent company of YouTube® and Google® and therefore a major Silicon Valley player, agreed as a political contribution to provide free tabulation of ideas and suggestions. Within a week, more than 48 million suggestions were received and tabulated. Based upon the inputs received, the design was finalized: the new flag of the ARC was to be blue in color. The central emblem was comprised of a silhouette of Karl Marx facing a silhouette of Charles Darwin; between the two silhouettes was a Festivus pole, a slender metal cylinder with a wooden X for a base.[2]

My sources tell me that a secondary task force made up of advertising agents was supposed to come up with a catchy nickname for the image (as in, "the Stars and Stripes") but as of this writing, had not come up with anything worth sharing publicly.

Citizens of ACNA, on the other hand, had to wait until April 1, 2029, to be reassured that their leaders had given serious thought to the matter of the flag:

---

2   The Festivus Pole is a nondenominational image of togetherness which was introduced to America during the mid-1990s, through a social documentary series called *Seinfeld*.

ACNA, Office of the President, April 1, 2029
Screenplay of President Christine Faith's Presentation On Voting for the New ACNA Flag

FAITH:

[walking down a suburban street past busy citizens: bakers, waving police officers, firefighters carrying a hose, hunters teaching their children to shoot, etc.] My fellow countrymen and -women: howdy, y'all. As we begin our existence as a new republic, we have a new identity. And so we need to create a new visual identity, in the eyes of the world. We need something that will say right away to the world, here's what I am and what I stand for. I know some of us miss the Stars and Stripes, am I right? To put it simply: Our nation needs a flag.

Our country was born so quickly that we created political change first. But now we need to take time to address the flag, since a flag is part of our identity. It shows the world who we are as a people and what we stand for.

Given the urgency of this issue, we have decided to shorten the normal consultation process associated with such an important topic because we need to have our flags hung with pride over our buildings, at monuments, and in our embassies throughout the world. Thus, my Cabinet assembled a committee of 30 — creative people, historians, and religious figures — and we gave them the task: to design a flag for our beloved Armed Christian Nations of America. Today, I am pleased to share their recommendations, which I will send to our legislative branch for review. It is my expectation that at a joint meeting of the House and the Senate next month we will be able to finalize the design. But tonight, I would like to share with you the committee's preliminary recommendations.

You all expect our flag to reflect our country's identity, culture and values. Well, as you can imagine, we started with red. [The screen dissolves into a red rectangle.]

Also, as you know, we are proud to be Christians. Therefore, we will have a cross on our flag. Something like ... this. [A cross fades in on the red background.]

We also have a commitment to our citizens' safety and freedom to bear arms.

[Images of rifles, dueling pistols, and revolvers fade in, and dance around the cross on the flag background.]

I don't think anybody is surprised by what I have described so far.

But I'm pleased to tell you that we have gone as far as we can with a design that reflects our values. As you know, we have a commitment to reducing the federal budget and also the tax burden on our hard-working citizens. Therefore, we will allow five lucky corporations to sponsor the country's official flag.

[Five gray circles, reading "Your Name Here" in the center, fade into view, strategically placed around the cross and one in the center.]

Each sponsorship will last five years and will cost each corporation $500 million. The price of sponsorship may sound rather high — but just imagine the level of exposure a flag would get. Imagine our flag flying over our embassies in New Delhi, Moscow, Beijing, Paris and London.

[the words "Artist's Rendering" appear at the bottom of the screen, and paintings of world buildings fade in and out, each with a red flag flying high.]

Frankly, we'll probably raise the price in the next round of sponsorship's open

enrollment period, so we encourage
interested corporation-citizens to send in
their applications as early as possible.

[shot returns to Faith standing in front of
the ACNA capital] I hope to be able to report
back in about three months. Meanwhile, please
don't hesitate to send your suggestions and
ideas to my office. Thank you, and God bless
the Armed Christian Nations of America.

Selecting the Capitals

As each country strove to make the move from temporary to permanent, each administration reevaluated the seat of their federal government.

President Castro and his administration had selected San Francisco as their capital, and they were not considering changing it. The mayor of New York City went so far as to take out a full-page ad in the *Times* asking for reconsideration, claiming NYC as the better choice. However, the administration would not be moved. President Castro said as much in a speech to his nation on February 14, 2029. He stood on a rocky outcropping on Alcatraz, with the San Francisco skyline behind him and a four-foot fiberglass sculpture of a heart next to him. Visible in the wide shot were his addressees: children from local public schools and their parents. Each child clutched a heart-shaped balloon.

Hola mis amigos; hello my friends; Namaste. On this day that we celebrate love of all kinds, I would like to talk to you about our new capital. I'm speaking to you from this beautiful windswept island in the San Francisco Bay. I am proud to call this place the capital of our new country.

I know that Mayor Nickleton would like us to consider her city for the capital, but I would like to say: Chelsea, you know we're good friends, and I admire your civic pride. But I bet you know as well as I do that San Francisco is really the best place for the capital of this new country. As always, New York will remain a very important city in this country and in the world. It's the greatest city in the world ... or at least, the second-greatest city. [Laughter.] But New York is part of our past. I'd like to say, New York represents where we came from, and San Francisco represents where we are GOING. [Pause for cheers.]

New York City has the Statue of Liberty. Ellis Island. The Triangle Shirtwaist Factory. Little Italy. The Empire State Building. Broadway. Harlem. New York City, which used to be, once upon a time, the first brief capital of a young United States. This represents where our country was born, and where immigrants streamed off of steamers and packet ships into our country and made it the melting pot, the melange of cultures and languages, that it is today.

Meanwhile, as the United States grew and fought and grew and fought some more, the country stretched farther and farther west. That spirit we call Manifest Destiny drew settlers and explorers across the vast prairies, seeking another ocean. San Francisco represents that reaching for something further, that chasing the dream. The spirit of exploration and innovation. The Gold Rush happened near here, in 1849. Levi Strauss invented ... jeans! [Pause for laughter.]

The flower children flocked here in the 1960s, looking for a new world of freedom and love. Two decades later, two men named Steve invented a computer that changed the world. Two decades *after that, two other young men created a little company called Google, that changed the world again. Less than a decade after that, thanks to Mayor Gavin Newsom, San Francisco became, however briefly, the first city in the country to legalize same-sex marriage. [Pause for cheering.] And just a hundred years or so after that, I hear San Francisco is going to become the headquarters of that bastion of further exploration, Starfleet Academy. [Pause for cheering.] Nerds, you feel me. [Laughter.]*

There's a reason why even our fantasies of the future cast San Francisco as the city on the cusp of tomorrow. And you should know that, Mayor Nickleton, since you went to Stanford. [Pause for laughter and cheering.]

We've all left our hearts in San Francisco. So, mis amigos, let us all celebrate love this day, and every day after, and may our new country create a better world for us all. Happy Valentine's Day, and namaste.

The ARC media absolutely loved the Valentine's Day speech, which touched on several sentiments and ideas at once. And even though New Yorkers grumbled about it (the *New York Times* published several grouchy editorials to that effect), the ARC public was, in general, relatively used to the idea of San Francisco being a hub for the kind of government they had always wanted: progressive socially, scientifically, and geographically — assuming that progress moves from East to West.

Meanwhile, in the ACNA, it was clear that not everyone was entirely pleased with the idea of Dallas as a permanent capital. Conservative pundits, commentators and bloggers complained that there was not enough public discussion about this very important decision. Conspiracy theorists theorized conspiracies. In other major Red cities such as Salt Lake City, Orlando, Cincinnati, Raleigh,

Charleston, and even Dallas's statemate Houston, tourist boards and private individuals paid for bus ads, online banner ads, social media sponsored posts, and billboards touting the delightful features of their own cities. A trend developed and many of the ads featured the phrase, "Why Dallas?" President Faith had since the country's official founding emphasized her commitment to widespread participation in the decision-making processes about the new government, and many ACNA citizens wondered snarkily on social media what had happened to that commitment. Thus, people were pleased to hear her address the nation on July 4th, about the country's new capital. Standing in the rose garden that had been planted on the roof of the temporary capital building, wearing a brilliant red skirt suit, she spoke directly to the camera in a single tight shot. (From a press release of the official text):

ACNA: Office of the President
FOR IMMEDIATE RELEASE: July 4, 2029
Text of the President Christine Faith's Speech to the Nation Regarding the Location of the Country's Permanent Capital
> *DATELINE: Dallas, July 4th, 2029. President Faith said, "My fellow ACNA citizens: howdy, y'all. As you are aware, when our glorious new country was created, one of the first things we had to do was to decide on the location of our capital. We only had a few days to make this decision. At that time, we decided that given the circumstances, Dallas was the natural choice. We took advantage of a generous offer by the Ross Perot Estate that provides us with favorable terms for a handful of buildings which have served as our temporary capital since January. However, it has always been a priority of ours to identify a permanent location for the great capital of this great nation. We formed a commission of highly knowledgeable people — sociologists, geologists, civil engineers, and religious figures — and gave them the task of researching the perfect location.*

"There were several factors we asked them to consider as they completed their research. First, a capital needs to be easily accessible by plane, automobile and train. Not just for those of us in government, but for all our citizens. Anyone in our great nation who wants to should be able to come visit our new government, look around, take a tour and see how well it works, this thing we all made together.

"The location must have a mild climate. There's no problem that we can't solve, but with summer days in Dallas routinely over a hundred, even a hundred and ten degrees, and with the hurricanes and tornadoes that happen so frequently nowadays, the outside atmosphere is not as pleasant as it could be.

"More than anything, a capital city needs to represent who we are as a nation. The city as a whole should represent, with its people, its buildings, its surroundings, and its overall ... "vibe" ... the values that our country holds dear. Today, I am pleased to tell you about the commission's final recommendation: the site of the Armed Christian Nations of America's permanent capital will be [pause for effect] ... Branson, Missouri.

"Perhaps many towns in the ACNA fulfill those three major requirements. There are plenty of cities that are centrally located, easily accessible, temperate, and generally representative of our values. But one important fact about Branson is that it's the site of the world's 10th-largest theme park. Branson will provide our hard-working government officials with wholesome appropriate recreational opportunities, without the vice and other distractions found in other major metropolitan areas. Centrally located, easily accessible, temperate, wholesome, and FUN. Look out, Branson ... here we come!"

Divided We Stand

Thus, by what would have been the 254th official birthday of the Pre-Separation U.S., the two new countries now had each either built or planned out: three branches of a federal government, a flag and accompanying branding strategy, a permanent capital, a national defense policy, and a set of guiding principles (snappily encompassed by the Three Gs versus the Three Ss). They had also created some radical new policies. The chart below is a comparison of the divergent policy changes that, between December 7, 2028, and July 4, 2029, the administrations of ARC and ACNA had either implemented already or promised to implement:

Changes in the First Half of 2029		
Issue	**Armed Christian Nations of America (ACNA)**	**American Republic of Compassion (ARC)**
Guiding Principles	• "God, Guns, and Greed	• "Science, Serenity, and Socialism"
Education	• Bible classes mandatory in K-12 and higher	• Commitment to teaching yoga and meditation in schools
Arms	• Firearms allowed on public land (national parks etc) and provided for temporary use	• Illegal for private citizens to possess firearms
National Defense	• Department of Defense becomes Department of War • Most (lower level) military operations outsourced to India's Maharaja Limited	• Dissolves Department of Defense and military • Treaty with ACNA, to swap scientific assets for military assistance if necessary

Changes in the First Half of 2029		
Issue	**Armed Christian Nations of America (ACNA)**	**American Republic of Compassion (ARC)**
Money	• Eliminates corporate income tax and sets 10% flat tax for individuals • Tax incentives for Stand-Your-Ground states	• Sets $100,000,000 cap on personal assets • Sets $1 limit on campaign donations
Public Health and Safety	• Mandatory K-12 firearms and self-defense training	• Begins to phase out the eating of animals over a 10-year period • Plans yoga and meditation in the workplace • Requires community service/volunteering time as part of employment

Though the countries' policies were different, so far the administrations were friendly towards each other. The two administrations made a conscious effort to show that the two presidents were on good terms, and that they were equally important and influential in world politics. At various international affairs such as summits and conferences, both presidents appeared together to represent the former U.S.'s interests, and there were numerous lavishly-staged press photo opportunities. At the 2029 Japanese climate summit, for example, Presidents Castro and Faith were photographed together in an official appearance with the Japanese prime minister. Meanwhile, their families were photographed together at Tokyo Disney. There were even pictures of the two First Gentlemen, Jack Gorbanski and Justin Faith, playing golf together at an exclusive Japanese course. (The vice presidents did not get along as well, although there was a video that went viral of a candid moment at a banquet: it showed a jovial conversation between Vice President (ARC) Wong's husband, Reginald Smith, and Vice President (ACNA)

William Winchester, both drinking bourbon and mutually admiring each other's sartorial choices, namely Smith's shoes and Winchester's belt buckle.)

Indeed, despite the possible national sibling rivalry that seemed like it might develop, so far the two countries and their leaders were doing just fine. The split appeared to be an amicable one.

CHAPTER SIX

The Separation Committee (Dividing the Assets)

WHILE THE TWO COUNTRIES WERE building their governments, distinguishing themselves internationally, and creating groundbreaking public policy, confidently moving forward, they also had to keep an eye on what they were leaving behind. The speed of the breakup of the old United States of America into two separate sovereign nations left many assets and properties under questionable ownership.[1] The most important were: military equipments and installations, federal buildings, national parks and monuments, financial assets and liabilities of the United States, and broadcasting companies. Thus, in April of 2029, a joint committee was created to deal with these issues. The committee was an "international"

---

1   My editor seems to think that I'm "mixing metaphors" by citing first sibling rivalry and then divorce. It took another discussion punctuated by the tossing of wine bottles to persuade him that both metaphors should be left in.

one, with members from both the ACNA and ARC governments. The members were: both vice presidents; secretaries from the Departments of the State, the Interior, and Commerce; and the Secretary of War (ACNA) and Secretary of the Bureau of Happiness (ARC). Additional experts were sometimes invited to attend and advise specific meetings depending on the nature of issues under discussion.

The Separation Committee decided to deal first with the most cut-and-dried issue: public land. The members of the committee decided that each new country would be responsible for the state parks, national parks and monuments in their respective states. Under duress, the ACNA government also agreed not to develop, subdivide or otherwise alter the natural environments of the national parks, for at least five years. The officials grumbled about natural gas deposits and other resources, but the ARC officials countered by describing those lands as "God's backyard," which was enough to begrudgingly persuade the religious ACNA officials and buy at least five years of nondevelopment. National institutions on what had been federal land outside of any state (i.e., in the District of Columbia), such as the Capitol Building, the White House, the Washington Monument, the Smithsonian and the Lincoln Memorial were leased to the Disney Corporation which was going to restore the buildings, repair the damage and then keep the whole area open as a giant historically themed amusement park, complete with rides so that visitors could truly enjoy their visit. Each of the three partners — ACNA, ARC and Disney — would get one-third of the profits.

Most difficult was the issue of the United States' military stockpiles. By the time of the Great Separation, the United States of America had been in possession of the world's most powerful military force, which also included a significant nuclear arsenal. After several weeks of intense negotiations, the committee decided that the military hardware, including equipment, vessels and all nuclear arsenals, would be divided equally, down to the item, between the two countries. Military personnel would be given a choice of either joining the ACNA Department of War or the ARC Bureau of Happiness, or else resign their commissions and return to their state of choice. ACNA quickly took over the possession of its share of military assets, including the nuclear arsenals. But things were a lot more complicated for the ARC, since the country did not want to have a military force and avowed it had no use for nuclear weapons. Thus, after several weeks of intense discussion at the Cabinet level, President Castro decided that his country would get rid of its nuclear arsenal and other military equipment completely. However, he was quite aware of the financial worth of the arsenal and its value to his new socialist country.

As for vehicles and vessels belonging to the ARC, they were disarmed and decommissioned, and then either converted to public civilian use (bolstering local ferry systems, for example), kept for non-military government use, or sold. The ARC government began converting some of its submarines and aircraft carriers into hotels and housing units, especially valuable off the coast of over-crowded San Francisco as both high- and low-income housing. Castro was persuaded to sell the nuclear armaments, since, after all, they would in all likelihood never be used. Given the fact that he had lived in San Francisco for many years and was well connected to Silicon Valley's business community, he decided that his country would auction its nuclear arsenal, using eBay as the most cyber-secure and field-tested method available to them. The bidding period lasted for one month. It opened on the first Monday in June and closed on June 30, 2029.

It was not merely a straightforward auction, however; potential buyers would submit their bids and the Separation Committee would consider each one. For obvious reasons, no anonymous bids were allowed.

Shortly after the bidding process ended, all the offers were made public. Twelve international governments submitted bids, including the ACNA. The three highest bidders, however, were: Saudi Arabia, the Chechen Republic of Ichkeria, and the United Arab Emirates.

President Castro rejected the offer from Chechen Republic of Ichkeria, given the uncertainty about the stability of the country and its connection to Russia. So for all practical purposes, only the bids from Saudi Arabia and the UAE were considered seriously. Both of these two countries' bids met the minimum requirements, but each of the bids offered a different financing structure. Saudi Arabia's offer was based upon repayment in oil; the UAE's offer was based upon payment in treasure and material goods, including vouchers for Dubai's world-renowned indoor shopping mall.

After an intense discussion, the Separation Committee recommended to President Castro's Cabinet a fifty-fifty sale of equipment to Saudi Arabia and the UAE. The deal with Saudi Arabia provided for very inexpensive gasoline prices to the citizens of the ARC until the full purchase price was paid, by which time the country would ideally have stopped relying on fossil fuels at all. The UAE's gifts and treasures were to be variously sold and their revenues used to solidify President Castro's socialist public policy.

The third major issue before the joint committee was the status of corporations that existed in the former United States. This issue was rather tricky, since a significant number of American corporations were incorporated in Delaware because it had the most corporate-friendly laws. But now that Delaware was a Blue state, there was a question as whether or not these companies would want to be governed by the laws of a Blue state. Corporations were given one year to decide whether they wanted to keep their incorporation status in Delaware or move to a Red State. The decision-making process could have been difficult. But an announcement by President Faith on April 1, 2029, made it quite simple.

My dear citizens, howdy, y'all. As you know, there has been a lot of discussion in the media about the future of our corporations, and the breakup with ARC, and all that. I'd just like to let you, my citizens, and any corporations who are listening, know that not only will we here in the ACNA be eliminating corporate income tax, as I've already promised, but we will also eliminate any possibility of criminal liability for our corporations. We in the ACNA know the importance of the corporation to the functioning of our country. This would allow our corporations to experiment freely in fields like medicine and pharmaceutical research, so they can make meaningful and quick advances without having to worry so much about being sued.

We don't believe that corporations should be criminally responsible for their acts of negligence, and we'll also take a hard look at the concept of tort liability and limit the financial awards that our court system can impose for a corporate act of civil negligence. This limit on corporate liability is essential if we want our country to assume leadership in the world. Corporations, we want you to know: ACNA is a great place to be!

Shortly after this announcement, many major United States corporations began the process of moving their headquarters to Dallas, Texas.

Moving a multinational corporation was complicated, however, which is why most chose to keep at least a subsidiary in the ARC. Though corporate liability was virtually nonexistent in the ACNA, the new country's morality laws made it even more difficult to do certain types of medical and pharmaceutical research, including anything having to do with fertility, conception and stem cells. Furthermore, a few major corporations' founders, especially those in Silicon Valley, objected to ACNA's policies on principle, and so chose to stay in the ARC.

Broadcasting companies kept their programming and broadcasting infrastructure; with television and streaming media all digital, citizens of the two countries had a choice of which networks and programs they would watch. Restrictions on programming content remained the same; however, the rating system was enhanced considerably, so that residents of ACNA could have advanced warning of any objectionable content. The beefed-up television rating system included new indications of religious content, as well as science content and specifically evolution content. Major broadcasters stayed put — CNN, however, negotiated to trade buildings with FOX: it negotiated an exchange of its headquarters in Atlanta with FOX's headquarters in New York City. Cable companies gleefully put together two separate cable packages, the Red package and the Blue package, thus forcing consumers who wanted both types of channels to pay twice as much per month for cable.

As for financial markets, New York City continued to host the New York Stock Exchange, and the city remained a financial headquarters. Many traders are unhappy with this, but there is too much financial infrastructure in New York to change anything quickly. As of this writing, the situation is ongoing.

Another important issue that needed attention was the nature of international agreements and membership in international organizations. Each of the two newly created countries agreed to abide for three years with all treaties, agreements and covenants that had been signed by the former United States. The trickiest issue was regarding the two countries' status as part of the United Nations. The United Nations charter had recognized the United States of America as a member of the United Nations Security Council. The Secretariat of the United Nations decided that both of the newly created countries were allowed to attend meetings of the Security Council. However, as the situation was too new to make any major permanent changes yet to the structure of the Council, the U.N. deemed that each one would only be able to cast one-half of a vote in the Security Council. In other words, both ACNA and ARC now need to agree with each other in order to be able to veto a decision of the Security Council. Many of the other member countries of the U.N. Security Council were happy with this decision, because it was expected that the two new countries would seldom agree on anything, and would therefore cancel out each other's vote. So far, this has indeed proved to be the case. As far as the United Nations Security Council is concerned, in some respects the United States has therefore effectively ceased to exist altogether.

PART THREE

Living With Change

CHAPTER SEVEN

Life Apart

Culture in the Armed Christian Nations of America

and the American Republic of Compassion

WITH THE PREVIOUSLY SHARED ASSETS more or less sorted out, and the two countries continuing on their own separate tracks, we can begin to examine, even in this short time, the effect that a new government and a new set of laws can have on a national culture. As you will read below, daily life in each country began to change in subtle but pervasive ways. Laws beget culture and culture in turn begets further laws.

After the turmoil of Separation and the confusion in its aftermath, people, as is their nature, wanted merely to return to a normal life. But what is the new "normal"? The previous chapter discussed mainly policy changes; in this chapter you will see how those changes trickle down to the populace and are folded into the mundane. Through the societal infrastructures of small and large businesses, personal technology, education and other everyday experiences, the new normal in each country becomes increasingly different from the old normal. If the 2028 election was indeed a "mandate from the people" as both new presidents continually avow, will the people actually enjoy this way of life they'd always wanted, this "new normal"?

Capitalism in the ACNA

On both sides of the borders, businesses were quickest to figure out the advantages in the new laws and new possibilities; one of the characteristics of an efficient capitalist country is that the economic system quickly responds to evolving public policies. In the ACNA, for example, major corporations made rapid business decisions to take advantage of the government's new policies about firearms. Web and TV ads for all kinds of companies began casually weaving firearms into their advertising storylines — not to mention the fact that firearm manufacturers themselves were allowed to advertise products directly, in print, on air and online. Businesses even used one of their most powerful tools: product tie-ins. Consumers were delighted by the Southern Oil Company's new marketing campaign: a free 9-millimeter handgun when customers filled their cars at any of the company's service stations throughout the country.[1] The marketing strategy worked: Southern Oil Company increased its sale of gasoline by 25% during the first week of the program.

As you can imagine, Southern Oil is but one example, and so within just a few months of the new country forming, guns became incredibly widely available, advertised widely and even given away. A few months more, and the government began to encourage gun ownership using actual financial incentives. The principle of self-determination meant that citizens should be both able and expected

---

[1]   ACNA citizens only; valid ID needed. One prize per fill-up per customer; subject to availability. Void where prohibited.

to help themselves when they are in trouble, which includes the idea that they should not have to wait for the police to provide protection for them. In effect outsourcing domestic security to ACNA's own citizens, the Department of Homeland Security provided rebates on the purchase of all types of firearms, including submachine guns. Many golf courses and country clubs began offering instruction in the use of machine guns. The owning and using of firearms became truly integrated with the country's popular culture, at all age levels.

Major corporations, having jumpstarted this cultural trend, could now increase their integration of their products with this new consumer craze. Among those companies that most cleverly capitalized on the zeitgeist was the Christian Morning Breakfast Company, which began to include colorful small — yet functional — firearms in its boxes of cereals. The company's revenues rose by 45% shortly after the introduction of this new marketing concept.[2]

Capitalism in the ARC

Though ACNA seems like the more likely place for capitalism to exploit government policy, ARC was not immune either. Business and technology merely provide people more of what they want, in order to make money. In this example, the policies in question are environmental in nature — though they have unintended consequences in the business sector, as seen in this report broadcast on CNN's evening news on June 2, 2029:

MARK MADSON:
And finally, tonight: I think this falls
under the category of Weird News, don't you,
Jeanine? Yesterday, at a national meeting of
the country's mayors, there was a national
crisis at the top of the agenda: Dog poop.

---

2 But there was also a 45% increase in incidents of cereal killings.

ARC environmental protection policies have made the manufacturing and sale of plastic bags illegal throughout the country. As a result, plastic bags are very hard to come by.

There are some bags that make their way here, mostly smuggled over the border through towns close to the ACNA. But these "genuines" are very expensive and not everyone is able to afford them.

Of course, "bio bags" made from agricultural waste are readily available — but according to one dog owner's gripe, "They're just not the same."

In Santa Monica, California, one group of dog owners has decided to stage a quiet protest, by not picking up poop. This protest is hardly popular with the legions of unfortunates who accidentally step on it, tracking it into their cars, homes and offices.

This in turn has spawned a counterprotest: people without dogs are putting together petitions, trying to get dog ownership outlawed. Their argument: how is it compassionate to allow human beings to own other creatures in the first place?

And it's not just Santa Monica. All over
the country [images of cities] — New York;
Boston; San Francisco; St. Paul, Minnesota;
Boulder, Colorado — wherever there are
people who love their dogs, these small-
scale protests and counterprotests are
occurring.

A surprising number of fistfights and other
altercations now happen daily between dog
owners and non-dog-owners. The anti-dog camp
wants recriminations, but it is difficult to
trace excrement to a particular dog without
eyewitnesses. DNA testing is expensive and
not without a time delay. Counterprotesters
are even petitioning to make neglecting dog
poop a felony.

Well, it's a dog-eat-dog world, Jeanine.
I'm glad I have a cat. [laughter.] And now,
let's throw it over to Scott, who's got the
weather.

Corporations soon recognized the problems with banning plastic
bags and rushed to come up with palatable and profitable solutions.
Shovels, scoops, plastic boxes, all manner of specific novelty items
began to appear on shelves. As usual, one corporation in particular
was thinking outside the bag. Only two weeks after the first dogfights
began appearing in the news, one could read in the June 22, 2029
e-edition of *High-Tech Weekly* the following short news item about a
new product:

"Appeale Corporation is working on an app that will allow individuals to determine the ownership of dog poop and therefore trace the owner. This would require taking a picture of the excrement samples; the infrared camera scans the sample for a unique chemical signature, and the app compares it to a national databank of registered samples, which will be one of the steps required when owners register their dogs with local authorities. The app may also be expanded to work on other animals, such as cats, birds, rabbits and chickens, but Appeale is still building those databases."

As proven just above, technology's function in society is to meet — and even anticipate — the needs of the citizens. Its effects are to guide those citizens further into a situation where those technologies actively *create* further needs, until the technologies themselves become such a part of our lives that it is unimaginable that we ever lived without them. Just as the telegram, the automobile, the phone, the television, the computer, the mp3 player, the smartphone, the smartwatch, the driverless car, the drone, have each in turn become seamless parts of our lives, these new countries are developing technologies that will magnify, and then further shape, the culture of their citizens.

Technology in the ACNA

Even in the Pre-Separation U.S, many cities and municipalities had passed legislation legalizing the principles of Stand-Your-Ground. After ACNA was created, the majority of its cities and states passed additional Stand-Your-Ground legislation. However, the patchwork of different laws and regulations proved confusing, as the number of citizens with firearms increased. Thus, people cheered a set of new regulations, widely announced via the following Public Service

Announcement, produced by ACNA's Patent and Trademark Office. It debuted on web, TV, and radio on May 15, 2029.

ACNA Patent and Trademark Office
PSA Script: Patriot Series
First aired: May 15, 2029

[SEXY FEMALE VOICE WITH A TWANG] Coming soon from the Guns of America Corporation: a new state-of-the-art handgun to make life in our country easier. This handgun will have built-in Wi-Fi, and an indicator light which will blink red when it is an area covered by Stand-Your-Ground legislation. The light will be blue when there is no such an ordinance in force. Available soon in revolver, shotgun, and rifle versions. Also available for holster, or clip-on sensor, to add to all your existing guns. Remember: Red means hold 'em, and blue means fold 'em. The Patriot: Brought to you by the ACNA Patent and Trademark Office.

The "Patriot" series of armaments came out in August of 2029, and continue to this day to be bestsellers. Walking down any given street today, at least one in three ACNA residents one encounters is sporting some sort of "Patriot" holster, purse, backpack, carrying strap or tote bag — or one of the popular knockoff brand carriers. It also leads to a less-crowded morning commute on city streets, as the sea of blinking lights means it is likely unwise to bump into someone, however accidentally.

Technology in the ARC

Ideas of compassion and happiness are a bit more difficult to incorporate into technology, but in the ARC, we do see the two concepts mesh. One way is actually more of an anti-technology statement: the government enacted a Digital Consumer Bill of Rights, championed by Vice President Wong and signed into law amid great fanfare. The Digital Consumer Bill of Rights, among other things, made a strong statement that technology and media companies were not allowed to track the habits of online users without their knowledge or consent: not web browsing, not physical movements, not purchases, not television viewing, not location tracking. Further, it did not allow companies to assume an "opt-out" strategy, referring to that as a "deceitful practice." In order for companies to track (and by extension, sell) this information, they would have to receive the consumer's informed, knowledgeable consent. Also, spam email and phishing scamming was to be aggressively tracked and prosecuted.

Corporations were understandably peeved about being prevented from tracking their consumers, but they quickly adapted some strategies. Tech companies began developing apps for a personalized technological experience. "Are you feeling stressed and anonymous?" one web ad campaign read. "Do you want your day to feel tailored exactly for you? Do you want to be introduced to new products that we know you'll already like? Do you want to feel … SEEN?" Users could then download the app: AdMe. Once users completed a simple quiz, the app would replace all the ads they'd normally see with ads designed just for them — and featuring their favorite colors, animals, songs, celebrities, etc. Many similar apps popped up, actively soliciting users for information in exchange for a relaxing, delightful, highly personalized advertising experience — and it didn't just end with the web. Walking by a business that your app knows you would like will trigger a notification on your device; and if you should happen to encounter an ad in the physical world (a subway ad, a poster, a billboard), thanks to Augmented Reality you could raise your device and view the world through its camera instead: onscreen, those random untargeted ads would be replaced virtually by ones tailored to you.

Apps such as AdMe are very popular among young people in the ARC these days; they like to dress, share and compare their 3D avatars. And once you've created an avatar, it can appear in your ads unexpectedly, cavorting with your favorite celebrities or animals, providing a delightful peek-a-boo surprise.[3] Social media is full of screenshots showing youngsters who have caught a glimpse of their own avatar, text-exclaiming, "FoundMe!"

An even more direct way to affect a user's happiness with technology was not far behind. A Silicon Valley company received a patent for a new biotech device that could measure exactly that: by measuring blood flow, hormones, respiration and other patented secrets, the sensor could accurately measure an individual's level of personal happiness. This technology was quickly seized upon by the ARC government,[4] specifically by the Bureau of Personal Happiness. A press release by the Patents and Trademark Office on May 15, 2029, provided additional information about this new device:

> *The Patents and Trademark Office is pleased to announce that last week it approved of a patent for a new device developed by the Glaed Corporation designed to measure an individual's level of personal happiness. This device, the Personal Happiness Monitor (PHM), will be provided free of charge to all citizens of the ARC.*
>
> *The device consists of a microchip that is implanted in the shoulders of individuals and can communicate with smartwatches, phones and other personal devices. The device has an LED indicator*

---

3   Such apps are fiendishly intelligent: via these avatars, users are essentially advertising products to *themselves*.
4   It may have been actually commissioned by the government; records prove unclear.

light, visible through the skin like a futuristic tattoo, available in the consumer's choice of colors: Clear Sky Blue, and Deep Sea Blue.

With these happiness monitors in place, we can track a wide variety of data, to make sure that we're appropriately achieving the recommended happiness levels of all the people in our nation. By keeping track of personal variables such as age, height, weight, gender, ethnic origin, city, neighborhood and other customizable fields, we can microselect your personal recommended level of happiness, crafting a state that's tailor-made just for you.

If the level of your personal happiness should happen to fall below the recommended minimum, your wireless device can provide you with locations for the nearest meditation center, yoga class, dog park or other appropriate treatment center. And if your device's light blinks at the "critical" speed, other residents know that you're feeling unhappy and that they should rush to your aid. Brought to you by the Bureau of Personal Happiness: We have compassion for you.

Education

Arguably the best way to perpetuate a system of thought or government is to instill those values within the education system. Each country had a clear direction: ACNA tied its education system closely into religious education (having gone so far as to substitute the Department of Education with the Department of Religious Affairs, remember) and national security; the ARC tied its education system closely with compassion, of course, as well as mindfulness and personal happiness. As illustrated below, in the second half of 2029, these two countries' educational efforts veered off in very different directions.

Education in the ACNA

President Faith had always been fully committed to protecting her citizens on the micro scale, and on the macro scale: she was keen to deal with terrorism head-on. It was easiest to start with changing education at the graduate level. In May 2029, the Department of Homeland Security established a graduate training program to address international terrorism. It sent out a press release, and began immediately mailing glossy brochures to college students and libraries. From the press release:

ACNA Department of Homeland Security
FOR IMMEDIATE RELEASE: May 20, 2029
Secretary Steve Janney Announces New Graduate Institute

The Department of Homeland Security is pleased to announce the establishment of the Dick Cheney Graduate Institute for Advanced Interrogation Techniques. The program will admit 500 individuals each year. The Institute's curriculum will provide its students with an exposure to the theories, practices, and history of modern advanced interrogation techniques. In addition, participants will have an opportunity for hands-on training and internships.

The institute's curriculum will include advanced waterboarding, sleep deprivation, and other enhancement methods. The program will also admit overseas students from allies of the Armed Christian Nations of America. Graduates of our program will be considered for important government positions, and will be eminently employable in multiple fields, including law enforcement, correctional facilities, airports, private security, and even education.

Within a week of this announcement ten thousand people had applied online for the program's September 1 start — once the number cleared fifty thousand, officials stopped reviewing applications and instead instituted a lottery system for admission. At last check before publication, the program was thriving.

From the early days of President Faith's administration, and the number of joint press releases (and also the number of intra-government golf tournaments and weekend retreats), it was clear that President Faith and her administration were committed to teamwork and interdepartmental cooperation. The official Facebook pages of the departments as well as their individual pages were plastered with group selfies featuring the text, "Love thy neighbor!" Secretary Steve Janney and Pastor Secretary Elijah Robinson in particular had become fast friends, and earnest collaborators, and could often be seen together in Dallas bars, vehemently discussing important issues over beers. This culture of cooperation was reflected in the joint cooperation between the departments of Homeland Security and Religious Affairs. From a joint press release:

ACNA Department of Homeland Security
& ACNA Department of Religious Affairs
FOR IMMEDIATE RELEASE: July 1, 2029
Secretary Steve Janney & Secretary Pastor Elijah Robinson Announce New K-12 Curriculum Standards

> *As we begin preparing for another academic year, the ACNA's first full school year, we find it necessary to revise our joint positions regarding the content, scope and teaching methodologies in our K-12 grades, as well as in our colleges and universities, and the qualifications of individuals whose positions provide them with the responsibility to shape the future of our country.*

First, it should be clear to everyone in our country that the election was a mandate, and a call to arms. Our people have spoken, and have decided they want a Christian nation. It is in this context that in our country we will not waste our limited resources to teach world languages in our secondary schools. All we will be offering starting the next academic year is English. As King Charles of Spain noted several hundred years ago, German is used to talk to enemies; French which is used to talk to friends; and Spanish which is used to talk to illegal immigrants; but it is English which is used to speak to God. Yes, God speaks only English.[5]

Now to our second point. For too long we have sat back and allowed godless, amoral men and women to rule over us — but no longer. The Department of Religious Affairs will shepherd our citizens away from human conjecture and human-created laws to get back to basic truths: God's revealed word spoken in the Bible.

The departments of Homeland Security and Religious Affairs will jointly ensure that judges, police officers, and elected officials and, yes, college professors, adhere to proper religious beliefs and conduct according to God's law. Eventually, the two departments working together will replace all secular teaching with only information adhering to those laws that God gave us. God is not an elected official who only sits for one term. God is the sovereign

---

5   The most often-quoted, though incorrect, version of this quote is: "I speak Spanish to God, Italian to women, French to men and German to my horse." (King Charles V) However, this is apocryphal. Girolamo Fabrizi d'Acquapendente's 1601 *De Locutione* was published 40 years after Charles V's death, and it is the earliest known to have listed two variations of this quotation. The First: "When Emperor Charles V used to say, as I hear, that the language of the Germans was military; that of the Spaniards pertained to love; that of the Italians was oratorical; that of the French was noble." Another variation, and the closest to the press release, is, "if it was necessary to talk with God, that he would talk in Spanish, which language suggests itself for the graveness and majesty of the Spaniards; if with friends, in Italian, for the dialect of the Italians was one of familiarity; if to caress someone, in French, for no language is tenderer than theirs; if to threaten someone or to speak harshly to them, in German, for their entire language is threatening, rough and vehement." The lesson here is that language, in all senses of the word, is political.

eternal monarch and He knows what's best for us; we must submit
ourselves to His rule.

This announcement was craftily timed, since it was made in July, when the majority of teachers were on vacation from school, so they were mostly working second jobs and couldn't get together to organize protests. Language teachers were, of course, appalled at the announcement that no language but English be taught. Happily, the Department of War immediately announced it would be hiring language teachers, since foreign languages were essential to military and espionage operations. Many school administrations across the country scratched their heads, wondering how they would switch curricula so quickly, with only two months or so until the start of the new school year. Thankfully, the majority of textbooks available in the ACNA already fit many of the standards revealed in the announcement, but teachers would have to be retrained and curricula redesigned in order to satisfy new requirements. Since implementing such new requirements is often left to school boards or even individual schools, September was sure to bring a patchwork of differing and conflicting standards. Much like normal.

The second part of the announcement was widely held to be merely conjecture, for it offered no specifics on exactly how those named officials would be made to "adhere to proper religious beliefs." Further, given the number and variation of Christian-identifying denominations, "proper religious beliefs" was a matter to be debated further. As usual, in order to normalize it, most kicked the idea down the road.

ACNA: Education and Science

Some university professors in the ACNA — even Christian scientists[6] — criticized President Faith's government for not

---

6   Not to be confused with Christian Scientists.

emphasizing science education alongside the new religious education initiatives. In answer, Faith held a press conference announcing the implementation of a national science media education program. As she indicated in her remarks:

We believe in science not just for a few; but rather for the many. We believe that science should be used to address the problems of everyday life: science should be helpful, and easy to understand. Unfortunately, in the old United States, science and its uses were manipulated by a few to gain access to grants from agencies such as the National Science Foundation. Scientists received money — from the government! — to study ludicrous, irrelevant things. Jellyfish brains? Snail shells? Ice somewhere in Siberia?

Scientists were also exclusionary: they made no attempt to make science accessible to people or easy for them to understand. That is why, working with our ACNA scientific community, we have developed a program called "Science for the Masses." This nightly program will be aired on our national television networks and will translate complex scientific ideas and theories into everyday plain English.

President Faith did keep her commitment. *Science for the Masses* aired every night on Fox Network. But what was rather puzzling to scientists was the fact that the science was presented using the analogies of Bible stories and parables, and often the views of prominent scientists were even misrepresented to conform to biblical stories, or just plain misstated.

For example, an episode first aired on July 30, 2029, was aimed at introducing the audience to Albert Einstein's theory of relativity. The program's host, beautiful blonde Heather Stanton, began by introducing Dr. Monte Newbury, a prominent professor of marketing, to present Einstein's ideas. The following is an excerpt from Dr. Newbury's comments introducing Einstein's contributions:

DR. NEWBURY:

Many people, when they think of Dr. Albert Einstein, think of him as the most important physicist ever born. That may be true. But did you know that Mr. Einstein was also one of the most innovative marketers of all time? As he writes in his memoirs, he recognized the power of marketing at an early age and began to apply it to his work as a scientist and in his personal life. He gives an example, from when he was working as a patent clerk in Zurich in the early 1900s. He had just gotten married, and needed to augment his patent office salary by working for a chain of barbershops to advertise their services. Using his scientific knowledge, he built a rectangular board which he carried on his back as he walked throughout town, during his lunch break. The board contained the following few words (but, of course, in German):

[Photograph of Einstein wearing sandwich board appears. Sandwich board reads, in English:

"If You Don't Want to Look Like Me, Get a Haircut Every Two Weeks"]

DR. NEWBURY (CON'T IN VOICEOVER):
His method worked! The chain of barbershops increased their revenue by 40%, relative to the previous quarter. And that is how Einstein's theory of relativity first got international attention.

ACNA: Education, Biology, and Human Rights

ACNA's official government stance is that abortion is immoral and against the country's religious sensibilities. The new government outlawed abortions, without exception. Abortion clinics were turned into Crisis Pregnancy centers, doctors were prohibited from performing abortion procedures, and it was even against postal regulations to forward any mail or advertisement from Planned Parenthood or similar organizations. Indeed, even to possess such literature became a misdemeanor.

The country's leaders were well aware that to avoid abortion, women needed to be educated about how to avoid pregnancy in the first place. Secretary Pastor Robinson installed abstinence education into public schools and universities, both in the religious studies portion of the day and also as part of Health and Biology classes. The government officially advocated total abstinence until marriage, when the only acceptable contraceptive method was the Rhythm Method — which happened to be completely free. However, due to the coy and embarrassed tone of most Abstinence Ed classes, many people's takeaway was that married couples needed to listen to Rhythm and Blues during sexual intercourse to avoid pregnancy. The country's leadership very quickly realized this problem, since the pregnancy rate increased drastically.

Television was a logical place for ACNA citizens to seek answers, but human sexuality was "too hot for TV" and *Science for the Masses* refused to touch the subject. The next logical source of guidance was religion. Thus, at the urging of the Department of Religious Affairs, every Sunday in almost every church throughout the country, and on television, ministers devoted part of their sermons to providing guidance about how to avoid unwanted pregnancy. Not wanting to further specify on such a delicate topic, Secretary Pastor Robinson left the details open, and thus the quality of this advice varied from one church to another and from one minister to another.

One minister in southern Mississippi, for example, Reverend Bubba Grant, made copies of a guide that was in use around 300 A.D., providing advice in how to avoid unwanted pregnancy. This advice, which had been widely accepted as the first scientific and Christian method, indicated that to avoid pregnancy, women needed to wear a rabbit's foot around their neck during their menstrual period. Any births that resulted from the failure of this method were officially attributed to user error, and women were chastised accordingly.

Education in the ARC

As mentioned in a previous chapter, President Castro thought so highly of education that he placed the secretary of Education just behind the secretary of State in his Cabinet hierarchy. His secretary of Education was the dynamic and cheery Dr. Kimberly Bagan, and she had ideas about how to improve the education system in this new country. Dr. Bagan has dual Ph.Ds in Education and Sociology from Yale, and she had long written about national education problems in the Pre-Separation U.S. Now, she could start with a clean slate, and she had the power to make some useful top-down mandates.

To announce some of those mandates, Dr. Bagan recorded a Public Service Announcement with the puppets from *Sesame Street* (released on YouTube® and PBS®):

DR. BAGAN:

Hi kids, I'm Dr. Bagan. I'm going to tell you about some new things that will be happening soon in your school. Remember how all of a sudden one day you woke up in a different country, even though you didn't even move anywhere? Well, we think that's pretty neat, and we have some really cool plans to make our country even better than it was.

And these plans start with … you! That's right! Kids are pretty darn important! Starting very soon, there will be a new part of your school day: Mindfulness.

The mindfulness part of your day will have three parts: First is check-in, when your class will all talk to each other about how you're doing, so we can talk it out instead of fight it out. Second is yoga, which is a fancy kind of stretching that also lets you and your body get to know each other better. It'll help you run faster, dance longer, and feel happier. Third is meditation, in which you sit or lie quietly and think about your breath. It'll help you stay centered and peaceful … school can be stressful! Now, if you'll excuse me: [takes lotus position] Ommmmmmmmmm … [Puppets join her; fade to black.]

As the new school year started in 2029, schools across the ARC received their yoga and mindfulness training, and implemented the programs immediately, with so far very positive results. The ARC also took advantage of assets gained in the Separation (National Science Foundation, National Endowment for the Arts, etc), to increase science and arts funding in schools across the nation, even restoring arts education and physical education to every K-12 school, many of which had lost those programs to lack of funding. It also increased the school day by a few minutes to allow for longer recess times, which was universally praised by biomechanists, teachers and children alike. Otherwise, there were no major structural changes to the education system, although major changes may be pending as of this writing.

ARC also used the media, as ACNA did, to reach out to a wider audience. One notable innovation: Dr. Bagan joined President Castro in strongly advocating for yoga and meditation for adults as well as children. Therefore, at the beginning and ending of the workday, CSPAN-ARC began to broadcast *Yoga Time*, a 30-minute yoga session conducted live by Dr. Bagan or one of her department colleagues. Residents of ARC could roll out their mats and perform yoga in the workplace with their colleagues, following along with the secretary of Health and Well-Being as well as the ARC legislators on the floor of the Congress, which happened to have a great view of the Bay. Businesses large and small were highly encouraged (and incentivized with tax breaks) to give workers their yoga time.

Business Time: ACNA, Unions, and Privatization

Another of President Faith's campaign pledges had been to increase the productivity of American business. This was an idea that no one could disagree with. Everyone wanted a more efficient economic system — how could you not? But what was not clear was just *how* to increase productivity.

Often, an increase in productivity happens when jobs are automated; replacing human workers with machines can make simple or repetitive tasks run more smoothly and efficiently. Instead, the Faith administration announced federal mandates to cut worker salaries, and reduce benefits such as retirement and health care. This signaled to private sector employers that they could start fighting in earnest against labor unions.

In addition, the government began to cut costs at the federal level by privatizing certain essential systems that used to be run by the government. Citizens were not happy. The ACNA media was strangely quiet about the resultant unrest, though the international media picked it up and ran with it. A report on Al Jazeera International on August 15, 2029, summed up the situation. From the official transcript:

Allan Shepherd: Yesterday, there were major demonstrations in Dallas and throughout the Armed Christian Nations of America's major cities. Like these people: in Dallas, this group of teachers, alongside children and their parents, were protesting the Faith administration's stated intent to privatize the entire educational system from kindergarten through college. Or these people: these New Orleans college students and recent graduates were protesting outsourcing, which leaves only low-paying jobs which do not provide health benefits or retirement.

Might organized labor help ACNA citizens negotiate for health benefits and retirement plans? Not for long. Recently, on a Friday afternoon before a long weekend, President Faith's Legislature outlawed unions and made union membership a felony. Even now, according to un-named sources, closed-door hearings are happening in the old capitol building in Dallas and in the new capital in Branson, Missouri. According to one inside source, all hearings begin by asking the witness, "Are you now, or have you ever been, a member of a union?"

Approaching autumn of 2029, what with privatization, layoffs and other ACNA economic policies falling into place, income inequality had already widened in the ACNA. The number of unemployed and homeless residents had skyrocketed, and ACNA corporations were reporting record profits. European sociologists marveled that it had happened so quickly, citing the abolishment of corporate income tax. They also wondered what would happen when April 15, 2030, rolled around and ACNA would see the effects of the 10% flat tax.

Faced with mass demonstrations and scathing media critiques, the Faith administration announced a truly humanitarian policy, aimed at helping the rank-and-file citizens. Secretary Steve Janney formally announced the new policy on October 14, 2029, speaking in a megachurch in Atlanta that ran the county's largest soup kitchen:

> "Greetings, my fellow citizens. We at the Department of Homeland Security are of course always concerned about the safety and whereabouts of our hardworking citizens. Our job is to keep our homeland secure. Based upon the reports the department receives, we know that at times our citizens can go missing. Perhaps our citizens have had a few drinks after a long day at work, and they get lost getting home. Perhaps our children decide to run away from home, or worse — are kidnapped. The problem of lost and missing people becomes worse when our citizens live in areas which are not properly lit at night.

> "Therefore, starting November 1, 2029, in cooperation with our partners at the ViGill Corporation, we will initiate the "Safe Citizens" program: we will implant a free chip in each citizen's shoulder, so that we can track the whereabouts of lost citizens, and bring them home to their loved ones. This chip will emit a harmless

LED light visible through the skin — much like a next-generation tattoo. And as befits a country that is totally devoted to the concept of citizens' participation in government, each citizen will be able to personally select the color of his or her light: Proud Flag Red or Deep Blood Red."

At the end of his speech, he held up an example of the chip, red light blinking, and put one arm around the megachurch's pastor, and the other arm around a friendly looking, carefully selected homeless resident; both of them smiled and gave a thumbs-up to the camera.

ARC: Problems with Peace

As can be expected, life in the ARC was not totally stress-free. True, gradual implementation of a humanitarian system of socialism did reduce many people's sources of stress and discontent. Certainly, not having to worry about health care, jobs and housing does a lot to reduce one's anxiety and alienation. But life in the ARC was a lot more complicated than it appeared to a casual observer of the country's political and sociological evolution — as seen with the issue of the plastic bags. Perhaps exacerbating issues like this was another, more serious issue — with the police.

Nationwide, nearly 75% of police officers in cities and counties were being laid off. This was due to a spectacular drop in crime rates, caused in turn both by the banning of the sale of firearms (and the accompanying buyback program) and the availability of free physical and mental health care for everyone. Departments had many fewer calls, and too many officers just sitting around, so police department heads and city governments decided to cut their costs and lay people off.

Police layoffs caused in turn what truly became a national dilemma. Here was a group of highly trained officers who, due to no fault of their own, had lost their jobs.[7] The country's unemployment took care of them, but it was hardly the same wage they'd had before. Citizens were outraged on their behalf. Meanwhile, small issues like "PlasticBagGate" could not be mitigated as handily by police intervention, since the now much-smaller police departments could not handle the same level of crowd control, with decreased numbers on the police force. And what of the Castro administration's pledge to provide all citizens with jobs?

The crisis did not go unnoticed by President Castro's administration. After several days of deliberation, the president, with full support of his Cabinet, announced a major national initiative: under the umbrella of the Bureau of Happiness, Castro created the National Happiness Brigade. According to Castro, in remarks from his Alcatraz office prior to enacting the order:

> *The Happiness Brigade will create a more compassionate society, on the street level. The person-to-person level. Officers in the brigade will be able to fulfill all those calls for which, pre-Separation, there was just no time. An elderly lady needs help going shopping. A child needs help getting a cat down from a tree. A group of tourists need directions. All these things and more are the reason why most police officers went into that line of work in the first place, no? Of course, there'll always be a little crime. But now we can finally have uniformed officials whose job is to make our society happier and better.*

The brigade members' task was both reactive and proactive. They would help people who reached out to them, but they were also to monitor the populace's happiness levels, and ensure that everyone was engaged in activities that accentuated personal happiness. Those who, for one reason or another, were below happiness standards were

---

7   Also, more alarmist commentators pointed out that these were the only people in the ARC who had been trained and authorized to carry firearms.

referred to the municipality's Happiness Enforcement Centers where they would receive appropriate treatment, depending on their level of unhappiness. Happiness Enforcement Centers offered massage, acupuncture, chiropractic, dance classes, yoga, Pilates, cannabis, trampolines, games of catch, and many other physical and mental therapies, depending on the needs of those admitted. As people made additional suggestions, HEC offices hired more staff. The laid-off police officers were automatically transferred to this newly created National Happiness Brigade, or what people jokingly began to call the "Peace Force." A national crisis was averted.

In a little less than a year, both countries had made some drastic changes, and averted some major possible crises. I have summarized the changes in the second half of 2029 in the table below:

Changes in the Second Half of 2029		
Issue	**Armed Christian Nations of America (ACNA)**	**American Republic of Compassion (ARC)**
Business	• Cuts worker salaries; reduces retirement and healthcare benefits • Criminalizes labor union membership • ARC corporations move headquarters to ACNA	• Implements yoga and meditation in the work-place • ACNA workers move to ARC for benefits and education • Initiates Jobs for All
Education	• Forbids teaching of evolution and other scientific concepts that contradict Bible • Begins to privatize education system	• Restores arts education and physical education to every K-12 school in the nation • Free education for all through 4-year college
Science	• "Science for the Masses" premieres	• Increases school funding for science and technology

Changes in the Second Half of 2029		
Issue	**Armed Christian Nations of America (ACNA)**	**American Republic of Compassion (ARC)**
Public Health and Safety	• Outlaws abortions; implements mandatory abstinence education	• Implements free mental and physical health care • Implements happiness monitors; creates National Happiness Brigade
Unrest?	• Nationwide protests over privatized education system • Nationwide protests over criminalized labor unions	• "PlasticBagGate" • Demonstrations over laid-off police officers versus promise of jobs for all

Both countries have faced an unhappy public, and though each administration has managed to smooth over the changes by changing policy to appease public opinion, I fear that internal peace may be temporary. The speed of policy change may well be outpacing the adaptability of citizens, even though the changes seem to be those that the people have always wanted.

If life inside each country is experiencing upheaval, how much stranger must life on the new borders be?

CHAPTER EIGHT

Life on the Borders

ITH THE GREAT SEPARATION IN action, merely a cursory examination of the country's new map makes clear that the sheer mileage of international borders was for both countries greatly increased. What's more, the new borders were all between states that, while always having been different states, had recently been part of the same country. Because of the vastness of the North American continent and the nature of the U.S. federal system, many of the changes made by the ARC and the ACNA were felt to varying degrees, depending on how far residents lived from the border of the opposite country. Because the state borders had not been as well-marked as the U.S's international borders, there are many, many cases of towns, businesses and even houses that are now in two different countries. Understandably, there was basically no standardization of practices for monitoring these borders from country to country or even from region to region across the continent.

An account of life on the borders could fill another whole book, and would no doubt be much stranger than fiction.[1] Plus, many of the cross-border operations have good reason to remain secret and anonymous, and it is difficult to gain their trust. Regardless, I present here at least a sampling of life on the borders since the Great Separation.

One surprising thing about Post-Separation life is that tourism has actually increased. People are now more curious about the other states now that they're actually a part of another country — now that they seem even more different than they were before. It's also the perversity of human nature not to be interested in something until after it's gone. Tourism advertising increased on both sides of the border, with the ACNA running campaigns such as, "Come visit Flyover Country, and see what the fuss is about!" or the ARC's campaign, "Life looks good in Blue."

More people than ever began visiting "exotic" places and national parks: New York City, the Rocky Mountains, Santa Fe and Taos, San Francisco, North Dakota, the old Washington, D.C., amusement parks … People were visiting their old homes or their friends and relatives as well, getting "the real scoop" on life in the other country. And international travel increased: journalists poured into the country, of course, but also businesspeople, anxious to figure out what was going to happen in the new economic climate(s). International tourists also came in droves, whether to gloat over the downfall of the United States at last, or just to finally come see what the fuss was all about, especially now that the tourist boards of both countries were advertising some great deals.

Travelers is one thing, but what about the people whose homes were on or very near to the borders? People living in those border regions Pre-Separation were accustomed to free passage across the

---

1   This reminds me to speak to my editor about another book deal.

borders, as free as sometimes literally crossing the street. In many cases, residents had previously been unaware of where the actual borderlines were. Many people worked and shopped across the state line from where they lived, and traveled back and forth several times in a single day.

With so many new international borders, most of which had never been previously marked or enforced, it remains unclear what local police and local businesses should do about differing regulations. Post-Separation, local border towns mostly operate along the same principles, on an ad-hoc basis, trying to leave things as much like "normal" as they can.

The gulf between laws in the ARC and ACNA, however, is expanding rapidly, even in just these few short months: in all ARC states, for example, firearms have been outlawed — but in ACNA states, firearms are common and practically mandated. Cigarettes are much more expensive on the ARC side than they are in the ACNA — but most states in the ARC sell recreational marijuana. The ACNA side has shooting ranges; the ARC has yoga studios. The ACNA side has NASCAR; the ARC side has sexual health clinics. In the ACNA, you can buy a gun. In the ARC, you can get an abortion. Ideologues or no, people have wants and needs that the "wrong" side of the border may be better able to provide them.

As I stated, local police and government officials are not sure how they should be dealing with the flow of people. There has been no resolution as far as requiring passports for international travel between ARC and ACNA, though there are factions on both sides that are clamoring for it. In lieu of passports, driver licenses will stand in; some local governments are passing regulations requiring casual checkpoints at major roads.

Some local governments have even instigated a Red Tax or a Blue Tax for certain commodities, or even local businesses in general: locals of the ARC would pay a certain price for something, but someone with an ACNA driver license would pay an added percentage. This

ID confusion has the potential for more serious consequences than just taxes: in the case of the Southern Oil gun giveaway, for example, gas stations were supposed to check IDs to make sure that only ACNA residents were eligible for the promotion. But as anyone who was once a teenager is aware, fake IDs are not terribly hard to come by. Predictably, the market for false and expired drivers' licenses has gone through the roof. Questions of allowable "dual citizenship" for people who own homes in multiple states, or those who work across the border, have yet to be resolved on the federal level, though both Supreme Courts have cases pending.

Thus far, the border towns have remained remarkably peaceful, due mostly to people's inertia, and the "you scratch my back, I'll scratch yours" attitude. The people who live there are the same people who have always lived there, and they behave the same to their friends, neighbors and colleagues. I have, however, sat in many border-town bars and restaurants, listening to the conversations around me, and I have learned some interesting things.

Some people in the ACNA are jealous of the "easy" lifestyle of people in the ARC, with free health care and secure jobs. Some people in border towns in the ARC have smuggled firearms across the border — not to use them, but because they feel unsafe living so close to a country so rife with weapons.

Some people belonging to certain religious denominations feel more comfortable joining a congregation over the border because of their order's particular values — I once sat in a burger joint surrounded by a cheerful busload of Quakers en route from their homes in Ohio to their regular meeting in Michigan.

It's apparently very easy to smuggle marijuana over the border into the ACNA, and hand it off in a border-town bar (I've been mistaken for a client more than once). I've been asked whether I have an "extra ID" for sale. At the same time, everyone I've encountered on both sides close to the border has been exceedingly polite, friendly and willing to chat.

To me life on the border feels like an uneasy peace, though I have nothing to base that on but historical record. It does, however, give me hope for an eventual two-state solution between Israel and Palestine. And, frankly, a slight fear of war in North America.

CHAPTER NINE

Separation or Divorce?

AS I AM FINISHING THIS manuscript, a question resonates throughout the world: in the ACNA, in the ARC, in the U.K., in Russia, in India, France, in Mexico, China, truly all over the world. Everyone wants to know whether the division of the United States into two republics is permanent, or simply a temporary hiccup caused by a unique set of circumstances in 2028. If this separation is indeed temporary, when would the U.S. return to the previous structure? If the bifurcation is permanent, what would happen to the previous treaties, alliances, and international agreements that had involved the United States of America?

I don't think anybody has a definitive answer to these questions. The only thing that seems clear is that the citizens of these two new countries are largely content in their new nations. Yes, there has been mass migration of families and individuals from one country to another. But that should have been expected because, as we discussed, the differences between the ARC and the ACNA were becoming ever more irreconcilable. If the division of the former United States is temporary, then one would expect that something needs to be corrected before the two sides come together — perhaps a rectification of some of the ideological polarization that caused the division in the first place. But, studying what has happened in each of these countries during the past year, there is very little evidence that this has taken place.

Indeed, a review of the major initiatives in these two countries suggests that various government actions in these countries during the past year have magnified the differences between the citizens of the two republics. It would be very difficult to tell people who have carried guns to work and school they can't do this anymore. It would be extremely difficult for an individual who has been getting completely free health insurance to understand that not only is it no longer free but he can't even buy it because of a pre-existing medical condition.

How could a country that has relied on religion and biblical stories return to science, to biology and to chemistry? How could a college student who thinks of Albert Einstein as a marketing expert accept him as a physicist whose theory of relativity (and many other fundamental scientific contributions) changed our understanding of the universe? How could a country that believes our planet was created in six days understand the complexity of our biological evolution? How could a nation that so embraces a certain truth be told to reject it and believe in a new one? The road to separation must be one way, for it is both dark and narrow; there is no room for a turnaround.

Thus, as I finish this book, I am able to answer a question I raised in the preface. Yes: the division of the United States of America into two independent nations, the Armed Christian Nations of America and the American Republic of Compassion, is both real and permanent.

The only question I am not able to answer at this time is: Why did it not happen earlier?

John Doe, Ph.D.

AFTERWORD

I SUBMITTED MY COMPLETED MANUSCRIPT to the publisher about 4 months ago. As I understand, the book is almost ready to be printed. However, there have been developments during the past four months that I think have some impact on the ending of this book. I feel compelled to share my revised insights with the readers.

About two weeks ago, Mandy Nasser, civil-rights lawyer, community activist, and former U.S. presidential candidate (see Chapter 4) attended a rally in Havana, Cuba. She was the guest speaker at a major event organized by the Occupy Havana Movement, a campaign very similar to one in which she was involved in the United States in 2008.

It seems that the resumption of diplomatic relations between Cuba and the United States, which began some 15 years earlier during the presidency of President Obama, has had some very serious impacts on Cuba's economy and social conditions. Diplomatic relations began slowly between the former communist state and the

Pre-Separation United States. However, capitalists from all over the world saw Cuba as a "new open market." It has become a destination for many cruise lines, and tourists flock to the small island in large numbers. Capitalism and Pre-Separation-U.S. style democracy have flourished in Cuba, which is beginning to have some of the same partisan problems the U.S. had some 20 years ago (see Chapter 3).

So it is not surprising to know that the organizers of the Occupy Havana Movement asked Mandy Nasser to be their keynote speaker on May 1, 2030. Her remarks were published by the Cuban newspaper *El Nuevo Herald* the following day:

> *Dear friends, I am honored to be your speaker today on this important day: International Worker's Day. On this date in 1887, mass labor protests in Chicago and in other countries led to the implementation of an eight-hour workday. It was a great victory for workers in the United States, England, France, Russia and many others.*

> *I speak to you, Cuba, but also to the citizens of my former country, from this neutral location. As many of you know, I have been carefully observing the two Americas that grew out of the Great Separation. I had no high expectations of the government of the ACNA. After all, one of their founding principles is Greed. So I am not surprised or disappointed that the government is a front for the country's rich and famous. There, everything is for sale, including votes of the elected officials. Even its flag has advertising on it! [Boos and jeers from the crowd.]*

> *But my greatest disappointment is what has happened in the American Republic of Compassion. Despite the best intentions, government is government. According to last week's investigative report by Al Jazeera America, the Glaed Corporation, which is implanting chips in ARC citizens to monitor their "happiness,"*

is owned by the same multinational parent company as ViGill Corporation, the company implanting chips in ACNA citizens in order to track their "whereabouts." Additionally, it seems that both companies are providing the governments with personal data related to their citizens. And both companies are, directly or indirectly in the case of the ARC, funneling huge sums of money toward political candidates and elected officials.

I'm sure many of us have read George Orwell's classic novel 1984, a story about a dystopian future world controlled by massive totalitarian governments. Well, my friends, Orwell's prophetic view has come true. We are indeed on the threshold of a new world order in which Big Brother Corporations monitor and control us. Is the former United States, thinking itself now two separate, independent countries, really just being duped by a massive mega-corporation mining our lives, our very bodies, for information in exchange for filthy lucre? [Boos]

And countries all over the world, countries such as Cuba, look to the former United States for guidance! If this Glaed/Vigil corporation is indeed multinational, how many other countries in the world are under its spell. We must be vigilant; we must stop this encroachment on our basic human rights.

Join me, my friends y mis amigos, in saying, "I am mad as hell, and I am not going to take it anymore!"

Judging from the cheers following her speech, and the speed at which it went viral, it is likely that many are unsettled with the directions in which these two countries have evolved. Ms. Nasser, by inference, seems to believe that essentially nothing of substance has changed, and that the real state of being which ACNA and ARC citizens have gotten used to is *not* the implementation of their real ideas and values in their two ideological utopias, but rather the state Pre-Separation U.S. was headed for at the point of Separation: corruption, internal espionage and authoritarianism. Is it reasonable to believe that the ACNA and the ARC are both being controlled by a semi-secret megacorporation, and that by accelerating their social change in order to pit the two countries against each other, that corporation is merely providing the people with a distraction so they don't notice what's actually going on?

I can honestly say that I don't know.

Many rumormongers in the Americas and farther abroad, entertain a more pressing and practical worry. Due to the countries' own policies, there are huge differences in military might between ACNA and ARC. Tension at the borders has increased in the past few months, especially with the recent arrival of ACNA's (outsourced) Indian soldiers along the ACNA/ARC borders to serve as the National Border Patrol, joining the more ad hoc local border patrol efforts. There have even been leaked reports (which may be spurious) from the ACNA's government that the ACNA is formulating demands that the ARC build walls along the ARC/ACNA borders, at the ARC's own expense.

The ACNA is definitely aware of the fact that its own residents are slipping back and forth across ARC borders in greater and greater numbers to take advantage of goods and services that are illegal in the ACNA: abortions, marijuana, same-sex marriage, etc. Certainly the number of homeless and destitute people in ACNA cities continues to increase, leading to both an increased crime rate and an increased rate of individual shooting incidents, both purposeful and accidental. And ARC doctors are curiously adept at treating gunshot wounds without acting surprised about where they came from. Perhaps the ACNA is growing jealous of its peaceful, educated neighbor? Perhaps ACNA officials are also anxious that while they themselves face a disgruntled and heavily armed lower class, their neighbor the ARC is flourishing without officially espousing religious values, and that the

ARC does not therefore deserve prosperity because it is populated by heathens and abominations?

Perhaps it is this situation that is spurring ACNA's public communications toward making increasing references to evangelism and to spreading the glory of a Christian God "worldwide." Could the most outlandish tabloid-style reports be true, that ACNA may be planning to reannex its closest neighbor, in a strange reverse echo of the American Civil War?

My sources in the ARC government also tell me that though the Castro government sold off its military supplies, it very probably did not divest itself of positively every single nuclear weapon. "Not that we would ever, *ever* use them," protested my anonymous friend. "But, you know, just in case. For protection." And with far superior scientific and technological resources at their disposal, who knows what other secret government projects (nuclear, biological, electromagnetic, supersonic) the ARC is working on, "for protection?"

Are President Faith and Vice President Winchester and President Castro and Vice President Wong and their governments forging brave new countries full of enterprising people who are at last liberated to make the world better? Or are they merely pawns in a sordid game run by international corporations that monopolize the military-industrial complex? Or ... both? And is Mandy Nasser a visionary, calling for an eleventh-hour revolution to save the fate of the world — or is she merely a rabble-rousing, fed-up liberal activist stirring up trouble in a misguided bid for attention?

As an individual I may speculate, but alas, as a proper historian I may only document. It may well be irresponsible to have speculated thus far. Regardless, tensions rise, people march, soldiers line the borders ...

Time alone may tell what may become of us. I can but fulfill my function and continue to observe our future as it unfolds — whatever that future may be.

John Doe, Ph.D.

APPENDICES

APPENDIX ONE

Country Relocation Algorithm

[Ed: Or, as popularly referred to:
"What's the Color of Your Soul?" survey]

[Representative examples of the official relocation quiz distributed nationwide.]

Country Relocation Algorithm

On a scale of 1 to 5, in which 5 indicates strong agreement and 1 indicates complete disagreement, rank each of the following statements:

The world was created in 6 days.
 1   2   3   4   5

Americans are biologically superior to other nationalities.
 1   2   3   4   5

America is the world's superpower because it is so chosen by God.
 1   2   3   4   5

Americans have a moral duty to intervene in other countries when they so choose.
 1   2   3   4   5

Americans should be able to carry firearms whenever and wherever they choose.
 1   2   3   4   5

Foreign nationals in the U.S. without a visa should be returned to their countries.
 1   2   3   4   5

Foreign nationals who are in the U.S. and who have children who were born here should be allowed to stay in the U.S.
1   2   3   4   5

Global warming is an ideology promoted by air conditioner manufacturers.
1   2   3   4   5

The government should abolish the Medicare program.
1   2   3   4   5

The government should abolish the Social Security program.
1   2   3   4   5

The government should not offer single-payer health insurance.
1   2   3   4   5

The government should not regulate energy-producing companies.
1   2   3   4   5

There is no threat to our environment.
1   2   3   4   5

There is no phenomenon called global warming.
1   2   3   4   5

Gays and lesbians will go to hell.
1   2   3   4   5

Everyone should pay the same tax rate.
1   2   3   4   5

Corporations should not be taxed.

   1   2   3   4   5

Unions should be outlawed.

   1   2   3   4   5

Abortions are immoral and should be outlawed.

   1   2   3   4   5

America is a Christian nation and that should be reflected in its public policy.

   1   2   3   4   5

* * *

The quiz ended with the following declaration:

"Congratulations! You have completed the test. Fill out your complete and correct contact information below, and press "Send" (only once). In fifteen to twenty business days, you should receive a relocation packet in the mail if applicable."

[Individuals whose total scores were in the top 25% would be automatically citizens of the ACNA; people who scored in the lowest 40% of the scores would be automatically citizens of the ARC. These two groups would be given financial assistance to relocate. Individuals who scored between those two levels had one year to decide in which country to declare citizenship, but these individuals would not receive any financial assistance for relocation, in effect representing a penalty, popularly known as the "Wishy-Washy Tax."]

APPENDIX TWO

A Country Divided

B Y THE END OF THE presidency of Barack Obama in 2016, the Red-Blue divide had widened to the point that the United States of America, one of the world's greatest and most stable democracies, was nearly broken: structurally, spiritually and politically. On every major issue political parties held diametrically opposing views, with nearly equal support, bringing the country to a standstill. While in a democracy it is not unusual to have differing points of views on current issues, what was unique and disturbing about the political environment of early 21st-century America was the extent and the purpose of these divisions. At times, parties created opposition simply for the sake of disagreeing with the other side. Weakening the other side had become an end in itself, and a major goal of each side's legislative agenda. The theory was that if the other side was weak, it could not get its agenda approved, and that would be a triumph in itself. The defeat of an opposing policy was just as celebrated, if not more so, as the win of a friendly policy — not exactly a recipe for getting things done.

Except for a few politically naive politicians, there were virtually no attempts on either side to compromise. Having consulted polls and read other media from pre-Separation times, I have determined that the following were the top dividing issues between the Reds and Blues. Interestingly, many of these most divisive issues were also those that are addressed in the country's foundational document, the Constitution of the United States of America:

The Role of Religion in a Democratic Society
Social Darwinism vs. Biological Darwinism
Second Amendment: The Right to Bear Arms
Immigration Issues
Healthcare Policy
Environmental Protection and Energy Use
Human Rights (abortion rights, civil rights, LGBTQ rights, etc.)

In the next few pages, I will try to summarize the essence of these disagreements and their consequences for Americans and for what came to be known as the Great Separation.

Darwin, Religion, and Monkeys, Oh My: The Role of Religion in a Democratic Society

The laws of God, the laws of man,
He may keep that will and can;
Not I: let God and man decree
Laws for themselves and not for me;
And if my ways are not as theirs
Let them mind their own affairs.
Their deeds I judge and much condemn,
Yet when did I make laws for them?
— A. E. Housman (from "The Laws of God, the Laws of Man")

"Without morals a republic cannot subsist any length of time; they therefore who are decrying the Christian religion, whose morality is so sublime and pure (and) which insures to the good eternal happiness, are undermining the solid foundation of morals, the best security for the duration of free governments."
— *Charles Carroll, signer of the Declaration of Independence*

"And I have no doubt that every new example will succeed, as every past one has done, in shewing that religion & Govt will both exist in greater purity, the less they are mixed together."
— *James Madison, letter to Edward Livingston, July 10, 1822*

"Congress shall make no law respecting an establishment of religion, or prohibiting the free exercise thereof[.]"
— *From the First Amendment of the United States Constitution*

With the ratification of the Bill of Rights in 1791, the American Constitution provided for the separation between Church and State. Whatever the personal beliefs of the Founding Fathers (the truth of which is up for debate and fundamentally unknowable), they recognized the importance of keeping religion out of the political process. The First Amendment stated that there should be no laws establishing religion, nor prohibiting people from practicing their own religion. The amendment reflected concepts articulated both by James Madison (main author of the Bill of Rights) and Thomas Jefferson. Until fairly recently, it was still plausible that espousing such a view[1] — that is, championing the separation of Church and State — could actually increase one's chance of being elected president. These views of Madison and Jefferson were eloquently reflected in

---

1   Though that oft-mentioned phrase does not actually appear in the Constitution, the First Amendment states: "Congress shall make no law respecting an establishment of religion, or prohibiting the free exercise thereof."

a speech given by then-presidential candidate John F. Kennedy — who would become the first Catholic president — on September 12, 1960, to the Protestant leaders of the Greater Houston Ministerial Association:

> *I believe in an America where the separation of Church and State is absolute — where no Catholic prelate would tell the President (should he be Catholic) how to act, and no Protestant minister would tell his parishioners for whom to vote — where no church or church school is granted any public funds or political preference — and where no man is denied public office merely because his religion differs from the President who might appoint him or the people who might elect him.*

> *I believe in an America that is officially neither Catholic, Protestant nor Jewish — where no public official either requests or accepts instructions on public policy from the Pope, the National Council of Churches or any other ecclesiastical source — where no religious body seeks to impose its will directly or indirectly upon the general populace or the public acts of its officials — and where religious liberty is so indivisible that an act against one church is treated as an act against all.*

> *[...] I do not speak for my church on public matters — and the church does not speak for me. Whatever issue may come before me as President — on birth control, divorce, censorship, gambling or any other subject — I will make my decision in accordance with these views, in accordance with what my conscience tells me to be the national interest, and without regard to outside religious pressures or dictates. And no power or threat of punishment could cause me to decide otherwise.*

> *But if the time should ever come — and I do not concede any conflict to be even remotely possible — when my office would*

require me to either violate my conscience or violate the national interest, then I would resign the office; and I hope any conscientious public servant would do the same.[2]

Although the U.S. Constitution prevents the government from the recognition of an official religion, by the late 20th and early 21st century the religious right began to erode that separation. Evangelical preachers began to found small, exclusive, family-led Christian universities with the purpose of training America's future Christian political leaders: Bob Jones University, Liberty University (founded by Jerry Falwell) and Oral Roberts University to name a few. Many governmental agencies began to display statues of Jesus or the Ten Commandments. It was difficult for even the U.S. Supreme Court to figure out where to draw the line. Two separate U.S. Supreme Court cases, both heard in 2005, concerned the display of the Ten Commandments on public land. In *Van Orden v. Perry*, the court found the display to be constitutional, but in *McCreary County v. ACLU*, the display was found *un*constitutional. Perhaps emboldened by this federal indecision, displays got more prominent and more personal: crosses began appearing on the walls of offices, and many municipalities began their official meetings with Christian prayers. This erosion of the separation of Church and State became more widespread and more political after September 11, 2001[3] when a group of terrorists attacked the World Trade Center in New York, and the Pentagon in Washington, D.C. Since the terrorists were Muslims, an expression of Christian faith became an act of patriotism and thus a major justification for considering the United States to be a "Christian nation," and trying to unite Church and State instead of separating them.

---

2   From "Address of Senator John F. Kennedy to the Greater Houston Ministerial Association, September 12, 1960." John F. Kennedy Presidential Library and Museum official transcript; http://www.jfklibrary.org

3   The actual historical date of the event now mostly referred to as "Nine-Eleven."

This evangelical fundamentalist Protestant viewpoint and the renewed urgency it generated allowed these religious views to enmeshed with the official Red political platform. The fundamentalists believed in the literal interpretation of the Bible; therefore, God created the earth in six days, Adam and Eve were the father and mother of everyone, and the Earth was created 6000 years ago. They rejected Darwin's theory of evolution and objected to it being taught in schools. They believed that the American government had to be a Christian government. They barely tolerated the existence of non-Christian Americans. And they seldom accepted them as equal. In order to appeal to their base demographic, the Reds allowed their political platform to include enforcing the "truth" of these beliefs by law, and thus religious thinking became ever closer to official political thought.

The Blues, meanwhile, were busy solidifying their own official platform. Their faith lay in science. They believed in Darwin's theory of biological evolution.[4] They believed that life began in the oceans, and that once on land, life evolved into various species. They believed that the Earth was as old as scientists said it was: approximately 4.54 billion years old. They believed scientific evidence proving that humans' effects on the environment were responsible for the global warming that fundamentally changed Earth's weather patterns.

Blues also believed in the separation of Church and State. They felt religion was a personal issue and outside of the purview of government. Further, they believed that religion should not extend itself into government or public space in any way. Where the Reds believed that "truths" described by their Christian religion — the universe is 6000 years old, the dinosaurs existed only as fossils, humans could not have contributed to global warming — should be given as much weight, political value, and educational time as the scientific "truths" proposed by scientists, Blues believed that those

---

4   As outlined in Darwin's *On The Origin of Species*, 1859.

religious points of view belonged solely at home and in the private sphere.

I further argue that the Reds, while rejecting scientific Darwinism and its theories of biological evolution and the survival of the fittest, believed instead in social Darwinism:[5] That some cultures and civilizations were more advanced than others, and that not all individuals were equal to others. Some of the Reds believed that the white race was superior to other races but that some white cultures were superior to other white cultures.[6] And that it was appropriate that some cultures would naturally dominate others. More specifically, many Reds believed that Americans (and American evangelical Christians specifically) were chosen by God, and that because of their cultural superiorities, it was appropriate for them to dominate other cultures and countries. In effect, as President William McKinley stated before the American invasion of Cuba (and Hawaii) in 1898, it was part of the United States' "manifest destiny" to rule and govern other countries and cultures.

National controversy related to evolution vs. creationism had deep roots in American history. The debate garnered national attention in 1925 when a math and science teacher in Tennessee, John Thomas Scopes, was accused of having violated the Butler Act, which prohibited the teaching of the theory of evolution. The case (often referred to as the Scopes Monkey Trial) was tried by two of the country's most prominent lawyers. Clarence Darrow, famous for his defense of many notorious clients in the name of civil liberties, argued on behalf of the defendant and in support of evolution. His opponent was the well-known politician and three-time presidential candidate William Jennings Bryan, who argued on behalf of the State of Tennessee, and directly in support of the biblical notion of

---

5   As outlined in several societal theories starting in the 1870s; while they did use the phrases "survival of the fittest," it was their opponents who labeled them Social Darwinists.
6   I find it curious that the complete original title of Darwin's seminal work was: *On the Origin of Species by Means of Natural Selection, or the Preservation of Favoured Races in the Struggle for Life.*

evolution. The questioning devolved from legal arguments to biblical ones, with Darrow actually calling Bryan — counsel for the defense! — as a witness and questioning him on the scientific plausibility of biblical statements, asking him whether Eve was literally created from Adam's rib, and where Cain's wife came from. The jury took just nine minutes to deliberate ... finding for the prosecution.

Although from a legal point of view, the creationist side won the debate, the trial was an immediate media circus, and most of the media's ridicule was reserved for Bryan and the prosecution. Adding injury to insult, as it were, Bryan died in his own bathtub five days after the trial ended. Given all this aftermath, fundamentalist Christians, without their most famous spokesperson, retreated. Mainstream education institutions backed off on their suppression of the science of evolution. There were still those crusading for a ban on evolution in school, but public opinion had spoken against them. Those religious folks who wanted to proactively protect their children from exposure to evolution theory either home-schooled their children or sent them to religious schools. The debate over evolution never quite went away: during the latter half of the 20th century, the battle continued. The Supreme Court of the United States ruled in *Epperson v. Arkansas* (1968) that prohibiting the teaching of evolution violated the First Amendment because it advanced a certain religion (i.e., creationism) over others; then Louisiana passed a law requiring classrooms to spend "equal time" on "alternative theories"; the SCOTUS in turn ruled that law unconstitutional. The term "Intelligent Design" evolved in the 1990s, state boards of education developed "disclaimer" stickers about the "theory" of evolution for their textbooks, and on and on.

But then with the emergence of the Tea Party in the early 21st century, the debate over science and religion once again became a central part of the political agenda, both at the national and local level.

Perhaps most symbolically, the same school district in Dayton, Tennessee, that in 1925 fired Mr. Scopes for having taught evolution in his science class decided to make a very public statement on the issue of creation vs. evolution. The school district's elected board in early September 2026 unanimously adopted a new hiring guidelines for all of its new teachers. Recognizing that a four-year education may indeed poison the minds of future teachers, the school board decided to revise its hiring guidelines so that it would require only a high school diploma and two years of college education, which would then be followed by two years of missionary work or internship in a Christian church. Applicants for a teaching position needed to submit three letters of recommendation from a minister or other religious official. Applicants were also required to sign a pledge that they would never talk about evolution in any of their classes. And finally, all successful candidates had to pledge that they would never require their students to go to any library not pre-authorized by the school board.

Tennessee's teacher qualification guidelines were soon adopted by several school districts in Oklahoma, Alabama and Mississippi.

Second Amendment: The Right to Bear Arms

"A well regulated Militia, being necessary to the security of a free State, the right of the people to keep and bear Arms, shall not be infringed."
— *Complete text of the Second Amendment to the United States Constitution*

Various Supreme Court interpretations of the Second Amendment to the American Constitution made it legal for individuals to possess firearms. More specifically, the rulings protected the right of citizens to keep and bear arms, separate from the idea of their right to form a militia. Ratified as part of the Bill of Rights on December 15, 1791, this amendment was one of the most dividing issues of American society from then onward. The amendment was the subject of many judicial decisions and public policy debates. The controversy over the exact meaning of the amendment was questioned in print as early as six months later, by Tench Coxe: "As civil rulers, not having their duty to the people duly before them, may attempt to tyrannize, and as the military forces which must be occasionally raised to defend our country, might pervert their power to the injury of their fellow citizens, the people are confirmed by the next article in their right to keep and bear their private arms."[7] The general interpretation was that the right to own firearms extended to individuals, as a protection against the possible tyranny of government.

In the late 20th century (especially as firearms became increasingly powerful, automatic and dangerous), the debate centered on whether the Second Amendment protected an individual's right to own firearms for his own personal use, versus the collective right of the people to be armed as a militia independently of an organized government military. But the proponents of the pro-individual-rights interpretation of the amendment proved to be extremely powerful throughout the years, and they were able to limit the nature and the scope of the debate. It was considered un-American to question the legality or usefulness of a broad interpretation of the Second Amendment in 21st century America. Somewhat more pragmatically, gun and ammunition manufacturers contributed generously to political campaigns. It was political suicide for a politician to show any hesitancy about the constitutionality of any type of gun-control legislation. The consequence was that by 2028, more than 70,000 people were killed each year by guns in the United States.

In the early 21st century, guns began appearing in high schools and even elementary schools. In many schools, teachers carried handguns to class because they were concerned that students might bring guns to class and assault other students. Students started bringing guns

---

7   "Remarks on the First Part of the Amendments to the Federal Constitution," *Federal Gazette*, June 18, 1792

to school in case teachers accidentally tried to shoot them. By 2014, the first records start to appear of schools and universities making purchases of military-grade equipment for use on campus. Some college police departments purchased assault rifles and trained faculty in the use of handguns and machine guns. One college in California purchased a bomb-removing robot for $700,000. One school district in Southern California possessed a bomb-resistant armored vehicle. This famously caused a literal educational arms race, culminating in situations such as university armies and elementary school drill team practice.

Building off this broad interpretation of the Second Amendment, states began to adopt and adapt legislation called "stand-your-ground" laws, which protect the use of firearms if a person, in a place where he or she has a legal right to be, were to feel his or her life might be in jeopardy. The first Stand-Your-Ground law was passed in Florida in 2005, with heavy support from the National Rifle Association lobby, in a time when Florida had both a Republican-dominated legislature and a Republican governor — Jeb Bush. Other states quickly followed suit; 35 states had similar laws as of 2028. The Stand-Your-Ground law altered the definition of self-defense; previously, someone threatened on their own property had a duty to retreat first, and only shoot or attack when they had no other self-defense options left. Now without the "duty to retreat," a stand-your-ground law was used frequently by individuals to justify the right to shoot and kill anyone who might be perceived as directly threatening. Several cases involving the Stand-Your-Ground laws created national debates and controversies during the presidency of Barack Obama. Protests, demonstrations, and rallies proliferated around the country, in the wake of ever-increasing numbers of stand-your-ground related killings. But in the end, gun-rights advocates prevailed and no significant changes were brought about.

While Reds, the main proponents of gun rights under the Second Amendment, were able to control the legislative process in many states, there was considerable popular opposition to guns. Several federal legal challenges made it all the way to the state supreme courts and federal district court levels — nevertheless, very few of them were able to clear the U.S. Supreme Court. The issue for the opponents of the Second Amendment was not whether the right to bear arms was itself a constitutional issue. Rather, many anti-gun groups believed that it was time for another constitutional amendment to severely restrict the use of legally owned firearms. But these initiatives were blocked by a very strong and well-funded gun lobby in many Red states throughout the country. The NRA, the leading organization in support of Second Amendment rights, was one of the most powerful organizations in the United States: Its contributions to political candidates was a major source of campaign funds for those seeking office.

The Second Amendment had been a rather controversial issue in American society and would get national attention every time someone's use of firearms would cause a national tragedy. But what made it even more controversial was the advancement in technology and its impact on the availability of inexpensive — and hard-to-detect — handguns. This issue came to national attention in one now-notorious incident.

In 2022, a high school computer class in Beverly Hills purchased a three-dimensional printer (as many schools do nowadays) for classroom use. A small group of students began to use it at night to produce plastic handguns. They used these weapons for a streak of neighborhood holdups. However, the problem was than no one in the area had any actual cash in their wallets,[8] and thus the group of students, which the media referred to as the Beverly Hills Bandits (BHB), changed their targets. With plastic weapons invisible to metal detectors, they managed to rob a local bank and then the Beverly Hills

---

[8]   They wisely deemed credit cards too traceable for their purposes, and also they had their parents' credit cards. One described afterward to interrogating policemen that their escapades were "you know, for the thrill of it, daddy-o."

Pawn Shop on Wilshire Boulevard, where they were able to get away with several Oscar statuettes, before their Rolls-Royce (belonging to someone's parents) was apprehended by police.

Once the BHB members were apprehended, copycat crimes popped up everywhere, and with the increasing availability of 3D printers in the average school, districts in the late 2020s were forced to roll with the times and regulate instead of ban:[9] students were allowed to take their guns out only at recess, and never during sporting events.

Not on My Turf: Immigration Issues

The United States, since its inception, was a country of immigrants. The United States as a political entity was created originally by colonists from England; later immigrants came from all over the world. It was the flow of immigrants that facilitated the industrialization of America. The railroad industry, the backbone of American industrialization, for example, relied heavily on immigrants, many from Asia. East Coast factories functioned because of the availability of cheap labor supplied by new immigrants. Many came through official channels and obtained proper work visas, but many also arrived without official visas. The proximity of Mexico and its land border with the United States in particular provided for a significant flow of Hispanic immigrants, both legal and illegal. Undocumented workers very soon became a main source of farm labor and other cheap day labor. According to some estimates, by 2020, nearly 17 million illegal immigrants from Mexico and Central American countries lived in the U.S. Many of these people had lived in the United States for years, paid taxes, and had children who were born in the United States. Many of these people worked as day laborers or migrant farmworkers throughout the West Coast of the United States and were an integral part of the U.S. economy. But they lived in fear

---

9 Similar to the way that cell phones in schools were at first banned, then regulated, and finally unrestricted use won out.

of deportation and were often exploited by employers who paid them low wages and provided no benefits. Many undocumented workers had no transportation and had to walk or ride bicycles in all types of weather conditions to work. The Reds wanted these people deported, even though they worked in both Red and Blue states. Immigration issues would usually surface during election campaigns, would create a huge stir, and then afterward would be placed on the back burner until the next election.

In 2014, President Obama used his executive power to offer temporary "amnesty" to some of those undocumented immigrants: immigrants who had been in the U.S. illegally for at least five years could come forward, and if they registered and passed a background check they could be granted a stay of deportation and a work permit valid for at least three years. According to some estimates, some 5 million individuals benefited from this executive order. But the Republican Congress challenged presidential authority and filed several lawsuits to fight this Executive Order. In 2017, Donald Trump, then president, issued opposing executive orders that greatly restricted immigration, resulting in massive public unrest, and new court battles. It seemed that everyone in Washington knew that they had to do something about this issue. But no one had the courage or willingness to address the problem. So the immigration issue remained as part of the nation's political agenda throughout the 2020s.

One of the most recent vocal opponents of immigration reform was Senator McCrosky (R, AZ), who was elected to office in 2024. Soon after his election, Senator McCrosky made the immigration issue his main legislative priority. He introduced a bill that would require all legal residents of the United States to register with their local police department, where a lab technician would take a cheek swab and then upload the result to a national DNA database. After that it would be quite easy for police officers or other government officials to quickly determine an individual's residency status. Those whose DNA was not on file, for whatever reason, would be immediately deported. Though this bill did not pass, it had huge support in both the House and the Senate, and failed to pass by a very small margin.

Race: The Loaded Question

I feel I must touch on this topic, even if only briefly. In tandem with the immigration issue is the question of race in the United States: the issue that no one wants to talk about. "Race" is a murky topic, and the definition of race vs. ethnicity is tricky. One major racial divide in the United States happens to be whites versus blacks. Many residents of the United States, especially those who would identify as "white," would rather somehow forget that the slavery of African people existed even in Colonial America, that our country was founded by people who actually owned other people, and that between 1501 and 1865 the American slave trade brought over 300,000 people to a land that became the United States. Even free blacks were not considered citizens and could not vote. The ugly business of slavery was definitively outlawed by the American Civil War, the end of which stopped slavery in the Confederate states and also brought about the Emancipation Proclamation, freeing all the slaves in the nation. The 14th Amendment in 1868 gave African-Americans citizenship, and the 15th Amendment (1870) gave African-American males the right to vote.[10]

Just because African-Americans had been legally emancipated didn't mean they had a particularly easy time of it after that. The Reconstruction Era attempted to restore the civil rights of freed slaves, although people in the former Confederate states strongly resisted those changes, with both legislation and brutal violence. Red states had laws that enforced discrimination and segregation, trying to eliminate black voters from voter rolls by creating barriers to voter

---

10 At that time, only males had the right to vote in the United States. Except for the territories of Wyoming and Utah, which by 1870 had both given women the right to vote — although neither was a state yet.

registration — something that continued sporadically until at least 2020, under the guise of preventing "voter fraud."

Healthcare Policy

Among advanced industrial countries, the United States in the early 21st century had one of the most archaic healthcare delivery structures. While first-rate healthcare service was available, it was not within financial reach of many Americans. Health insurance was available to those who worked for major organizations. Self-employed individuals or those working for small businesses often lacked such coverage. Those who did have coverage would lose it when they lost their jobs. People with pre-existing conditions were systematically excluded from buying insurance, or had their policies canceled after they filed a claim. Given the soaring cost of health care, people with serious illnesses often lost their entire fortune when they lost their employment. Indeed, two-thirds of all personal bankruptcies were due to medical expenses. As early as President Bill Clinton's era in the 1990s, a number of attempts were made to create a single-payer insurance structure. But the Reds opposed it. Republicans did not believe that government should in any way be involved in providing or administrating health insurance. They wanted the private sector to be responsible for it. Then during the presidency of Barack Obama, after a national legislative battle, the Democrats were able to get a piece of healthcare legislation passed. But the Republicans challenged its legality, and tried on numerous occasions to defund the law in part or in whole. The Supreme Court ruled in the president's favor at the time. But the fight continued until 2017, when Republicans, who were now in charge of the presidency and both houses of Congress, began the process of systematically dismantling the Affordable Care Act, popularly known as "Obamacare." America once again became the only advanced country without a national health insurance system..

Environmental Protection and Energy Use

Environmentalism in the United States began in the 19th century, with people like John Muir and Henry David Thoreau lending their philosophical voices to the cause. Thoreau's *Walden* described the need for a relationship with the natural environment. Meanwhile, Muir successfully lobbied for Yosemite to become Yosemite National Park, the first national park in the United States. Later Muir went on to found the Sierra Club, in 1892. In the late 19th and early 20th centuries, people began to notice and worry about the extinction of iconic American animals, including the bison and the passenger pigeon.[11] The thread of environmentalism continued in America; Earth Day[12] was started on the first day of spring, April 22, 1970.

Environmentalism was not always linked so directly with industrial growth and energy use, but as the population grew and American prosperity grew with it, the direct effects on the environment and the economy became more obvious — to some. With the growth of the population — and the American auto industry — in the 1950s, it was nationally important for gasoline to be cheap and abundant. However, due to the availability of cheap oil from the Middle East, and robust American oil production, it did not become a problem until the early 1970s. There was an energy crisis in 1973, resulting from a perfect storm of factors. In January of that year, the American stock market crashed under the weight of inflation. A few months later, in August, the Arab-dominated Organization of Petroleum Exporting Countries declared an oil embargo for America, in retaliation for American involvement in the Yom Kippur War on behalf of Israel.

---

11 The passenger pigeon once flew in flocks of actual billions, but was hunted into extinction by Americans and the bird thought to be the last specimen died at the Cincinnati Zoo in 1914.

12 The official founder, Senator Gaylord Nelson, wanted to call the day "National Environment Teach-In" throughout his lifetime; Earth Day was suggested by a member of his organizing committee, advertising executive Julian Koenig, because April 22 also happened to be his birthday, which rhymed with Earth-day. Let history decide what the correct name should have been.

Oil prices quadrupled by December 1974, when the American stock market finally recovered from the crash. As a result of this energy crisis, industry began to create alternative solutions: Americans began to buy smaller European and Japanese import cars, and the American auto manufacturers responded by creating smaller and more fuel-efficient cars themselves; public transportation became more popular; innovators explored alternative sources of energy; there was a national campaign of conservation, including a national campaign by the Advertising Council with the tagline "Don't Be Fuelish."

But, the crisis also spurred the oil industry to increase American production, and when the crisis abated, prices fell again and Americans returned to normal habits. This cycle continued throughout the following energy crises of 1979, 1990 and the mid-2000s.

Americans did begin to notice the practical effects of industrial pollution, however, when smog generated by automobiles and industry began to darken the sky in major cities in the United States, and acid rain began to damage public buildings and monuments.[13] In industrial cities of the Northeast, smog generated by industrial plants affected water supplies, air quality and every aspect of life. In Pittsburgh, executives used to carry an extra shirt to work to change into at noontime because by that time their once-white shirt was all gray. As the price of foreign oil soared, American energy executives began to look for alternative supplies of energy. Nuclear energy plants were built throughout the country. But the cost was too high. So, there was a search for alternative energy. One of the strategies heavily employed in early 21st century by oil companies was a technique called hydraulic fracturing, or "fracking," which involved injecting a slurry of water and chemicals at high pressure down a well bore to fracture the rocks and release oil and gas trapped within them. Fracking also involved cyclic steam injection: pumping superheated

---

13 In 1962, biologist Rachel Carson published the book *Silent Spring*, which catalogued the effects of spraying the pesticide DDT, and questioned what the long-term effects might be on humans, animals, and the environment.

steam into underground seams to loosen and liquefy viscous crude oil.

Fracking was not an entirely new innovation; a patent for the ancestor of modern fracking was issued in 1866 to Civil War veteran Colonel Edward Roberts; he referred to the technique as the "Exploding Torpedo." Other early fracking attempts used nitroglycerin for their explosive charge. The 1970s and 1980s brought new technology and new thinking to the problem: George P. Mitchell figured out that fracking could release hard-to-obtain gas from dense shale, if the shale deposit already contained cracks. The technique continued to be refined, especially as demand for oil and gas increased while the availability of easy-to-extract deposits decreased. By the early 21st century, fracking experienced a huge boom, as an inexpensive strategy to increase oil and natural gas production. In such states as Texas, Louisiana and Oklahoma, fracking was used without much oversight or controversy. But it then began to spread to other states throughout the country. Soon, opposition to fracking surfaced because of its consequences for the environment: the process allows harmful gases and chemicals to escape into the air, and the water and chemicals used in the fracking process could easily seep into the local groundwater. In addition, a growing number of scientists believed that fracking could affect the geological integrity of regions and could possibly generate seismic activity in long-dormant faults with no recorded history of earthquake activity. This fear was intensified by an increase in the number of earthquakes in areas that had no history of such activity. In particular, in 2011, an earthquake registering 5.8 on the Richter scale got national attention because it damaged the Washington Monument a short distance from the White House and the U.S. Congress. Then in 2014, a 4.8-magnitude earthquake struck near Conway Springs, Kansas, while during the same week, magnitude 3.7 and 3.9 temblors hit Montana.

It was this increase in seismic activity in areas that had little history of earthquakes before fracking that sparked national attention.

Television networks had segments about earthquake activity and newspapers devoted pages to it. All this resulted in a congressional hearing in the House of Representatives to hear testimony about issue related to fracking and its impact on and relationship to seismic activity. The hearing took place in 2022 in the House of Representatives, the Subcommittee on Science and Technology, which was chaired by Congressman William T. Cannon from Alabama. The hearing lasted two weeks and included testimony from Pastor John Shultz, the head of a major congregation in Oklahoma City; John C. Sidney the CEO of Southern Oil Company; and Dr. Beverly Ghosh, the chair of the department of Geology at Caltech. The subcommittee's hearings were summarized in a report that appeared in the *Federal Register* on March 21, 2022. The hearing captured the essence of how Congress viewed environmental issues in general and fracking's environmental impact in particular.

Federal Register, March 21, 2022

Committee on Science and Technology, House of Representatives. Honorable Congressman William Cannon, (R-Alabama) chair of the committee provided closing remarks at the end of a weeklong hearing related to banning hydraulic fracturing.

The committee received testimony from a wide range of individuals, some of whom had financial interests in the fracking business.

Congressman Cannon thanked the committee's last witness, Dr. Beverly Ghosh, chair of the Department of Geology at Caltech. He acknowledged the receipt of her 350-page written testimony, which included computer simulation results and numerous charts and tables. Her reports concluded by stating that the materials used in fracking, including various chemicals, when reinjected underground could not only threaten the safety of underground wells, but could also lubricate ground fault movements, resulting in massive earthquakes, and possibly even produce explosions and earthquakes.

Dr. Ghosh's testimony included a report produced by the U.S. Geological Survey and university researchers, which showed that between 2010 and 2013, nearly 100 earthquakes greater than magnitude 3.0 struck the eastern part of the United States annually. A report conducted by Dr. Ghosh's own lab found that between 2013 and 2020, that number rose to 200 per year. This compared with only 20 per year in the same region between 1970 and 2000. The report linked the increase directly to the impact of injecting water deep into the ground.

Congressman Cannon sarcastically dismissed Dr. Ghosh's testimony about the geological and environmental impact of fracking by stating that: "God created this planet, and the universe. And only he can alter it." He further admonished the scientific community not to cause panic for "hardworking Americans" by falsely claiming that hydraulic fracking can contaminate groundwater and cause geological change and reactivate dormant fault lines. "The American people," he reminded Dr. Ghosh, "are tired of the atheistic scientific community which has forgotten the lessons the Holy Bible has taught us all: God created planet Earth for Man to live upon. He wants us to get the oil out of the ground."

He indicated that opposing fracking was un-American. He indicated that he would ask the Department of Homeland Security to look into the background of scientists who opposed fracking. He adjourned the meeting with a prayer and without moving to take any action on fracking.

There continued to be divisions among the Red and the Blue states regarding the environment. Was there a real danger to the environment related to population growth, industry and unregulated energy use? States were divided, and to some extent states could deal with these issues themselves, at the state or local levels. But some of the regulations were federal regulations and affected all states equally.

One issue that had divided not just state governments but also the states' electorates was the preservation of endangered species. A major recent incident that captured national attention was in 2019, when a moderate earthquake damaged State Route 60 in several places near the City of Industry in Southern California. The freeway connects several major cities to Los Angeles as well as to Arizona and the East Coast. It took several weeks before the California Department of Transportation was able to approve a contract to repair the freeway. But by this time, two endangered birds — a pair of California towhees — had created a nest in the crack in the freeway. When Caltrans engineers inspected the site to develop specifications for the repairs, they saw the birds, but did not think much of it. Except that the next day, the local newspaper published a photograph of the birds nesting in the crack. That photo went viral. Within hours, officials from the California Department of Fish and Wildlife, the state's agency responsible for protecting endangered species, visited the site and decided that the birds could not be moved until the eggs had hatched and the nestlings were on their own. Thus, the repair work could not begin and in turn, hundreds of thousands of individuals spent many more hours in their car taking alternate routes. Was it better to repair the road and further endanger the species, or was it better to preserve the birds while creating much more air pollution and wasted energy? The internet blew up over this single question. This issue accentuated the differences between the Reds and the Blues in regards to the centrality of environmental issues in people's lives and the role of public policy in protecting the environment.

Unions and the Minimum Wage

Beginning with the early 20th century, collective bargaining became part of America's economic landscape. The National Labor Relations Act of 1935 made it illegal for any private-sector employer to deny its employees the right to unionize. This act was fiercely opposed by the Republican Party at the time. Even government workers were allowed to unionize, as per an executive order by President Kennedy in 1962. Unions thrived for nearly 50 years, until the early 1980s, when the issue of productivity and labor costs became part of the national debate. This change of opinion took place during a period of economic recession, which had been accentuated by changes in the international arena and the gradual thawing of the so-called Cold War between the United States and Russia. Massive and relatively very cheap labor pools in China, India and other countries became available to American companies, and were heavily exploited by American manufacturing companies, draining American jobs as they became "outsourced," building factories overseas instead. Many people, particularly in large manufacturing states, began to criticize unions as the source of America's lack of competitiveness and other economic problems. The issues with the unions drew increased attention during cyclical economic recessions. In particular during the Great Recession of 2007-2012, the unions had become the target of Republican propaganda campaigns. Red political commentator and TV personality Bill O'Reilly for example, once blasted teacher unions as a group that "does not love America."

Unions that primarily provided protection for blue-collar workers became the scapegoat for governmental inefficiency. So in effect, by blaming the unions and organized labor for U.S. industry's lack of competitiveness, the Republicans attempted to create anti-union sentiment among middle- and lower-class Americans, traditional supporters of organized labor.

During the Obama administration there was an attempt to increase the wages of hospitality workers to $8 or $9 per hour in such places as San Francisco, New York and Los Angeles. But these efforts were opposed by both small firms and big business, which publicly labeled such measures as job killers (while avoiding the subject of profit margins). In sum, the Reds hated the unions; the Blues largely supported them.

Sexual Orientation

Homosexuality has been part of human history since the first Homo sapiens walked on Earth. It was part of the social framework in many world societies since ancient times. Nevertheless, Christianity, the dominant religion of the Reds in the United States, opposed homosexuality.

Sexual orientation was not a major concern of American political life until the early 1970s. At that time, because of the American Cultural Revolution of the 1960s, a byproduct of the Vietnam War, it became increasingly more acceptable to discuss one's sexuality. The Stonewall riots in 1969 galvanized the gay community to organize, and led to the first Pride parades in 1970. And as the idea of homosexuality became public, it became another dividing issue between the Reds and the Blues in the United States. The Reds maintained that humans had a choice over their sexual orientation and that homosexuals should not serve in the military or hold important political positions. In effect, the Reds viewed them as second-class citizens. Many Reds did not have a problem with discrimination against homosexuals, and they criticized the Blues for their acceptance of homosexuals and their willingness to provide them with equal protection under the law. In 2015, the U.S. Supreme Court ruled on *Obergefell v. Hodges*, legalizing same-sex marriage nationwide, which added fuel to the homophobic fires.

Abortion Rights

Abortion and birth control were controversial legal issues in America since almost its beginning. Anti-abortion laws started appearing on the books in various states starting in the 1820s. By 1900, it was a felony in every state, though some states had exceptions to make it legal in certain circumstances. In a 1973 decision, The U.S. Supreme Court in the case of *Roe v. Wade* and a companion case, *Doe v. Bolten*, ruled that a right to privacy under the due process clause of the 14th Amendment extended to a women's decision to have an abortion — thus making abortion fundamentally legal. In practice, these rulings and a few related judicial decisions allowed women to legally abort an unwanted pregnancy during the first trimester without any restrictions.

However, the ruling did allow the states to place regulations on abortion, and during the following years many regulations sprang up. In Red states, restrictions were so strong that it almost became prohibitive particularly for individuals with limited resources. In Red states, abortion clinics were boycotted. In several instances, physicians who had performed abortion were assassinated by people opposed to abortion who wanted to save the fetuses. Some political pundits felt that the abortion issue had become a very controversial aspect of political life and contributed to a gradual realignment of political parties in the United States after the *Roe v. Wade* decision.

Torture/"Enhanced Interrogation"

One of the guiding principles of American government since its inception was adherence to a set of fundamental principles, now called Human Rights, which in part included humane treatment of prisoners of war and individuals who were in police custody. Indeed, after WWII, the U.S. facilitated the convening of an international tribunal dealing with the treatment of prisoners of war. For two centuries, the U.S. was admired around the world for believing that there was a difference between a civilized world and a barbarian society. However, with the growth of the Red Culture in the U.S. there was a gradual erosion of these principles. Thus, by 2001, after the terrorist attack on New York's World Trade Center and the Pentagon, the CIA began to use torture as a means of getting information from several individuals who were arrested and accused of involvement in that and other terrorist plots. None of these individuals was charged with any crime. Yet, these individuals were held for many years, some for longer than a decade, and were subject to routine torture. The tortures they endured were labeled by some as worse than those used in Europe during the Dark Ages. These acts of torture were classified in "enhanced interrogation" files and kept secret from the American people, including many in the federal government itself. Approved by President George W. Bush and engineered by Vice President Dick Cheney, who served as its proponent in the White House, the tortures included such techniques as: Waterboarding, rectal rehydration, rectal feeding, electric shocks and other inhumane techniques, including the threatened use of a handgun and electric drill. A report published by the U.S. in December 2014 provided a summary of how torture was used. "Under any common meaning of the term, CIA detainees were tortured," said California Democratic Sen. Dianne Feinstein, who headed the U.S. Senate Committee on Intelligence, which published a 500-page study summarizing America's use of torture during the presidency of George W. Bush.

Despite the shocking nature of Feinstein's report, and the national outcry over the use of torture, many Reds still felt that the use of torture was justified. John A. Boehner of Ohio, the Speaker of the House, reacting to the news of the torture made public on December 9, 2014, said America's intelligence community deserved "our thanks, not an ideologically motivated report designed to undermine their work."

While many Reds approved of the use of torture, most Blues objected. They were appalled by the report and by how over 10 years, the American people, including members of Congress, were lied to by the CIA and even the Republican administration regarding practices involving "enhanced interrogation." The disclosure of the torture report did point out that President Obama had ordered a halt in the use of torture shortly after he was elected in 2008. The next administration, under Donald Trump, covertly reversed course on such tactics.

APPENDIX THREE

Timeline

A Brief Encapsulation
of the Rise and Fall of the United States of America

1607-1732: Kingdom of Great Britain founds 13 colonies on East Coast of the American continent as part of the British Empire. Periodically battles against France for control of American territory.

1754: Albany Congress: Individual colonial governments begin to work together. Northern seven out of 13 colonies send representatives. Declare intolerance of taxation without representation in Parliament. Discuss Benjamin Franklin's "Plan of Union": a confederation of 11 colonies, with a President-General appointed by the King of England. "Plan of Union" rejected.

1763: "Seven Years' War"/"French and Indian War" ends; France expelled from American continent. British Monarchy sole European power over North American East Coast.

1773: "Boston Tea Party": After British Tea Act allows East India Company to sell tea directly to colonies, lowering price significantly while adding a tax, small group of Massachusetts colonists destroy several tons of tea.

1774: In retaliation for "Tea Party," British pass "Coercive Acts," known to colonists as "Intolerable Acts." Aggressions between Britain and colonies increase.

September 5 - October 26, 1774: First Continental Congress; 12 of 13 colonies send delegates.

June 12, 1776: Second Continental Congress begins drafting Articles of Confederation.

July 4, 1776: Declaration of Independence adopted. (Famous enlarged copy not actually signed until Aug. 2nd).

September 9, 1776: Congress formally renames nation The United States of America (replacing the United Colonies).

November 15, 1777: Virginia becomes first state to ratify Articles of Confederation.

February 2, 1781: Maryland 13th and final state to ratify Articles of Confederation. Weak federal government made official.

1783: Revolutionary War ends. U.S. wins.

1787: U.S. Constitution signed and ratified. U.S. has an official system of government.

1791: Bill of Rights Ratified; first 10 amendments to the Constitution, including freedom of speech, separation of Church and State, and confusingly-phrased rights to bear arms.

1824: First presidential election in which the winner of the popular vote did not receive enough electoral votes to win the presidency. President John Quincy Adams elected.

1860-1861: Seven southern states vote to secede from the United States over their rights as states to continue slavery.

1861-1864: U.S. Civil War; estimated 625,000 to 750,000 Americans die. United States of America stays united.

1870: 15th Amendment to the Constitution grants African-Americans the right to vote.

1876: Second presidential election in which the winner of the popular vote did not receive enough electoral votes to win the presidency. President Rutherford B. Hayes elected.

1888: Third presidential election in which the winner of the popular vote did not receive enough electoral votes to win the presidency. President Benjamin Harrison elected.

1920: 19th Amendment to Constitution grants women the right to vote.

1925: Scopes "Monkey" Trial in Tennessee, show trial and media circus, ultimately finding for states' right to ban the teaching of evolution in schools.

1929: Financial collapse, leading to Great Depression. United States remains united.

1917-1918: U.S. involved in WWI.

1941-1945: U.S. involved in WWII.

1959-1975: U.S. involved in Vietnam War.

1962-1973: Vietnam War Protest Movement. *(Blue)*

1954-1968: African-American Civil Rights Movement. *(Blue)*

1969-1974: Gay Liberation Movement. *(Blue)*

1970: First Earth Day celebrated. *(Blue)*

2000: Fourth presidential election where winner of the popular vote did not receive enough electoral votes to win the presidency. Supreme Court decides the winner in *Bush v. Gore*. *(Red)* Media accidentally creates the terms "Red states" and "Blue states" in post-election coverage.

2005: First Stand-Your-Ground law passed in Florida, under Governor Jeb Bush. *(Red)*

2007: "Great Recession": housing market crash and economic downturn in U.S.; spreads globally. United States remain united.

2008: Self-titled "Tea Party" faction of conservative voters comes to prominence. *(Red)*

2010: U.S. Supreme Court passes "Citizens United," deregulating campaign contributions and donation limits. *(Red)*

2016: Fifth presidential election where the winner of the popular vote did not receive enough electoral votes to win the presidency. Hillary Clinton, the first woman to be nominated by a major political party to run for president, won the popular vote, but lost the election to Donald Trump who won the necessary electoral votes to become the nation's 45th president. *(Red)*

2021: Representative John D. Henry introduces constitutional amendment to replace electoral college with one nationwide popular vote for president.

2028: Highly contested presidential election (Faith v. Castro); **SEPARATION BEGINS!**

ABOUT THE AUTHOR

Dr. John Doe [Ed: Real name withheld for security reasons] was born in the Red state of Georgia. His parents were of mixed origin: His father was a native of Blue Oregon and his mother was from the Red state of Tennessee. Thus, at an early age, he faced conflicting views of reality and truth. It was this parental duality that instilled in him a sense of fairness and balance, which prepared him for an academic career.

Dr. Doe completed both his undergraduate and graduate work in history and political science at the First Universal College of Knowledge in New Zealand where he received a full scholarship for the duration of his studies, which he was able to complete in four years.

Upon graduation, he joined the faculty at the Las Vegas Institute for Advanced Studies in 2010. Dr. Doe has held visiting positions at several universities, including Princeton, Yale, Cambridge and Harvard. Dr. Doe's area of expertise, for which he is known internationally, is contemporary American history. He is the author of 23 books on American history and has published more than 150 journal articles. Recent works include the three-volume history: *Social and Political Thought in Nevada*, and the much-lauded *American*

Capitalism in Action: A History of Timeshare Real Estate and Las Vegas Casinos. He is currently working on a new book: *Mustang Ranch: An American Institution.*

A frequent commentator on national television, he divides his time between his homes in Las Vegas and New York City. When not writing or lecturing, Dr. Doe composes poetry for relaxation. He wrote the following poem after completing this book:

We are the Reds
We are the Blues
But we ain't got a clue

We are the Reds   We are for the Lord
If we must, we'll waterboard
So we can eliminate the non-Christian horde

We are the Blues   and We don't care
Just for a few
That's why we provide everyone
A free vaccine for the flu

We are the Reds
We are the Blues
But we ain't got a clue.